Criticism in Focus

THOMAS HARDY

Charles Lock

Bristol Classical Press

First published in 1992 by
Bristol Classical Press
an imprint of
Gerald Duckworth & Co. Ltd
48 Hoxton Square
London N1 6PB

A catalogue for this book is available
from the British Library.

ISBN 1-85399-007-8

Printed in Great Britain by
The Cromwell Press, Melksham, Wiltshire

Contents

Acknowledgements

It is a pleasure to acknowledge the generosity of my colleague, Michael Millgate; the ready sharing of his scholarship, and loans from his library, greatly eased my task. I express my thanks to Walid Hamarneh for bibliographical assistance, to Margot Thomas for the procession of words, and, especially to Linda Munk for critical advice and informed encouragement.

Heredity being what it is, this slight work insists on being dedicated to the memory of an earlier commentator on the theme, my grandfather, Major H.O. Lock (1879-1962), lawyer, soldier, author, and friend to Thomas Hardy.

C.J.S.L.

2 June 1990

Introduction

Thomas Hardy has been the subject and the focus of a vast amount of critical and scholarly writing. This book, while adding to the mass, is offered as a guide through the shelves of the secondary; it is also a commentary, part analytical, part polemical, on the situation of the critical tradition within aesthetic and political ideologies. As Hardy is being revealed, lined up, positioned, contextualized and re-historicized within the plurality of discourses that criticism now commands (or serves), we can point to the lag, to the institutional obstructionism, to ideological entrenchments, and we can anticipate. And it is that anticipation, of Hardy's centrality in a future criticism, that justifies the present exercise. For in surveying the works of scholarship and criticism written about Hardy it will be our purpose not to make assessments of intrinsic worth (for whence, now, comes such confidence of evaluation?) but, rather, to understand the symptoms.

Students of few other writers begin with such advantages, can avail themselves of such scholarly labour: two distinguished biographies (Millgate, 1982; Gittings, 1975, 1978), an exemplary bibliography (Purdy, 1954), the *Personal Writings* (ed. Orel, 1966), the complete letters (eds Purdy and Millgate, 1978-88), the personal notebooks (ed. R. H. Taylor, 1978), the literary notebooks (ed. Björk, 1985), numerous annotated editions of all the major texts. The obvious lack is of a 'definitive' edition of the complete works. When we remember that Hardy's published works came out of copyright only in 1978, we can hardly accuse scholars and editors of reluctance. Early on in his career (but not early enough) Hardy purchased a standard text, a work of literature that no writer should ignore – *Copinger on Copyright*. This is not

1

the space in which to insert an account of copyright as a determinant of literary reputation and critical endeavour: it is so blatantly massive that it has not borne thinking about. Macmillan served Hardy and the Hardy Estate very well. The general reader was not ill-served either: manic reprinting, without any resetting let alone renewing of type, does, after all, keep costs down. It is only the specialist who suffers – and liberal humanism thrives on such sacrifices to the notion of the general reader. Another factor of uncountable import but not specific to Hardy, so here alluded to merely, is the ratio between general and academic presses in determining literary status. The Clarendon Press, Oxford, initiated and published Purdy's bibliography in 1954, and went on to publish the *Collected Letters* in seven volumes (1978-88); Gothenburg University Press first published Hardy's *Literary Notes* – typographically a most expensive undertaking. The Clarendon Press was free to produce editions of Hardy's works only after 1978, when all other publishers were equally free. So far we have editions of *Tess, The Woodlanders*, and *The Complete Poetical Works* in three volumes, but little sense of a complete edition, and no sense, no intention even, of editorial overseeing and consistency through all the volumes.

This is far from regrettable. The notion of 'definitive', whether of text or edition, had faded before 1978; had such an enterprise been initiated in the 1970s it might now seem antiquarian. Another reason for the fractured or episodic relationship between Hardy's novels and scholarly texts concerns Hardy's readers. Do university presses take on lavish scholarly editions of writers whose works have ceased to command general interest, or do they actually bring about the decline in readership? One thinks of the Yale Boswell, the Clarendon Bunyan, even the Princeton Coleridge: the existence of these superlative editions has pushed out popular editions, editions that one might *read*. Hardy has not been thus entombed: it is presumably the astonishing demand for popular editions that renders a definitive edition impractical. What is a paradox in the classroom may not be so in the market.

First and last the focus of scrutiny, the place where all the incommensurables meet, is Hardy's popularity. This popularity has nothing to do with that of 'popular writers,' has nothing vulgar about it. We can be condescending about some of the uses, applications and exploitations, but of the reading of Hardy, in itself, there is nothing vulgar unless it be high-mindedness. In the past 50 years Hardy has spanned the entire range of readers as no other writer: there is a statistical consistency wherever we look, in GCSE and 'A' Level examinations, in doctoral dissertations, in lending libraries, in any bookshop. Not only in Britain but throughout the English-speaking world, and even in translation (with a massive statistical bulge in Japan), there is the same consistency. And there is nothing innocent, accidental or natural about this.

The academic study of modern literature has brought about the establishment of canons and rules of exclusion. As long as criticism saw itself as the assessor and arbiter of value it had to discriminate between 'literature' – books that had value – and other books, the worthless ones. The history of academic institutions tells us why such values cannot be manifest but must be hidden, awaiting demonstration. The deictic never justified a teacher's salary. Even where value is manifest it must be shown to be not exactly what it purports to be, but ironic or ambiguous. And 'ironic' is probably the commonest word in the academic jargon of Hardy criticism. Teachers have explained that Hardy did not 'really believe' in 'the President of the Immortals,' that Clym's 'Sermon on the Mount' is an ironic version of another's, that dramatic irony abounds, and that every coincidence throws an ironic light on freedom and destiny. Irony is the easiest of initiations. But it does initiate, divide those within from those without, and the teacher's role is, however slight, indispensable.

That is Hardy's gift to New Criticism or, as it should more accurately be named, the New Pedagogics. This was devised in response to the crisis in the humanities that occurred in the United States in the immediate post-War period, when the G.I. Bill gave to large numbers of returning servicemen the right to higher education. University teachers of English could not expect those students to have the traditional educational background and preparation, and both texts and methods were trimmed accordingly. Neither the novels nor the poems required much background knowledge for some appreciation and understanding; there is no extrinsic or esoteric body of information with which the reader needs to be acquainted. New Criticism's rigorous exclusion of extratextual information has had many absurd consequences: the reduction of *The Waste Land* to a discord of tones, the exclusion of W.B. Yeats' beliefs from his poems, the scandalous reduction of Ezra Pound to an episodic lyricist. The absurdity of Yeats' beliefs and the vileness of Pound's doctrine are notorious – as excuses for sticking to the text, for that mental inertia and disdain for simple curiosity that is the characteristic of modern educated taste. A New Critical reading of Hardy's novels can barely resist mention of the disparity between the author's charity and generosity of spirit, and Hardy's personal meanness that biography has presented to us. Such contradiction or impasse is, as it were, punishment for those who stray from the text.

Ideologically it is often important to maintain the wide, all but irreconcilable difference between the man and the writer – whether Hardy, Yeats, Pound or Eliot – in order to establish the separateness of literature. Literature is a discourse – we have been taught to suppose – separate from the psychological confusions of its writers, from the economic circumstances of its production, from the needs and demands of its readers. Literature exists above and apart from all that. The New Critical dogma is itself symptomatic of readers' needs and demands – that literature be a separate discourse, appropriate for detached, objective study, and that it give access to a world less squalid than that by which it is generated and in which its authors and readers live. The New Pedagogics could safely allude to the ideal, for it allowed no possibility of praxis. For such a programme Hardy was extremely well suited. Not only do his readers require no specialized learning (just that core curriculum from Aeschylus to Schopenhauer which is 'our natural birthright') but it has proven difficult for scholars to establish special concerns – of Hartmann's philosophy, or reform of the marriage laws, for example. Emphasis on particular causes or angles has not been fruitful. Hardy's texts are barely and insignificantly illuminated by research into philosophical and social problems, the conditions of agricultural labour, problems of access to higher education, or the study of historical sources for the Napoleonic Wars. What Hardy knows, he shares with us, leaving no remainder undisclosed. For the New Criticism there could be no stronger evidence for the self-sufficiency of the text.

Hardy offers few opportunities to scholars, and many to teachers. The best criticism has been of a general nature, sensitive, sympathetic, even committed, but not, in the formidable sense, scholarly. The majority of the good books on Hardy read as transcripts of lectures and seminars; the majority of the bad books bear witness to scholarship in the desperation of its impotence. One would not trust an amateur with Henry James or James Joyce: to speak with conviction of such writers presupposes a great deal of homework, a keeping-up with the aggregation of scholarship and criticism. In the field of Joyce studies there are no amateurs, only charlatans. Yet one cannot imagine the degree of intellectual deficiency that would render an essay on Hardy the work of a charlatan.

And so it is assumed that Hardy is the possession of the general reader, a writer by whom no reader need be intimidated. The critical literature – to mention only the works of David Cecil, J.I.M. Stewart, Irving Howe and John Bayley – enforces the assumption. Expertise, or specialization, does not pay. Yet behind this is something less simple, a problem that is beyond our current means of analysis. What mediates between Hardy and the general reader is not the critical or scholarly literature but the institution of teaching. Of all Leavis' failings – few major critics had more – none is as notorious as his exclusion of Hardy from the 'Great Tradition.' Of all the 'Leavisites' (by that graceless term denoting not 'disciples' but those of evident pedagogic filiation) few have sought to share or defend Leavis' estimate of Hardy.

Rather, one finds numerous gestures of reparation; recognition that Hardy does indeed belong to the 'Great Tradition', that he, more than James or Conrad, is the pivotal novelist between George Eliot and D.H. Lawrence. School examination syllabuses testify amply to this striking modification of a curriculum with which Leavis would otherwise have no quarrel. If Hardy was the blind spot at the very centre of Leavis' vision, then the curriculum which Leavis (together with the New Critics) did so much to shape, both in Britain and in North America, could not but admit Hardy, and admit him centrally.

Hardy's popularity with the general reader is therefore circumstanced. The 'general reader' has probably undergone at least secondary education, has been taught to find in literature what Hardy offers, and would regard the appreciation of Hardy as one of the benefits of education. Those same students are usually sceptical of, and dissatisfied with their teachers' claim that all great writers can be understood by means of the text alone. There was, after all, little enough to be enjoyed on such a tight budget. In the terms of Leavis and the New Criticism, annotation and apparatus were dirty words and looking up references became a covert operation. No wonder that Milton's reputation collapsed, that Spenser's was summarily ended; the Augustans obviously preferred to belong to no other time than their own, and Browning floundered. In each of these instances the poet was accused, not of making the reader work too hard or know more than is good for her, but of stylistic and rhetorical lapses. Context was deemed irrelevant, and where it was inescapable it was internalized as formal or stylistic error.

Such observations are now familiar, almost routine. In the present climate of literary study at conference-curcuit level, which has, despite much publicity, barely reached the undergraduate curriculum, let alone secondary education, all is otherwise. History and context now matter once more, not as aspects extrinsic to the text but rather as extensions of the text, of textuality. Literature is no longer perceived as a separate discourse but as one continuous with other discourses, deprived of its privileged exemption from the messy processes of getting and spending, producing and consuming. The current climate, whatever it may be labelled, could never be called pedagogic. It is not best suited for expression in the classroom. Dense, allusive prose is its characteristic medium. General readers keep out.

Against the critical approaches which have succeeded New Criticism the common objection is that they are too complex and obscure to teach. On the other side, it can be objected that New Criticism surrendered everything that was not pedagogically expedient. New Criticism, in its quest for pedagogical method, had little respect for things and facts as they are. Contemporary literary study is concerned with things and facts, excluding neither metaphysics nor epistemology, neither biography nor bibliography. Hardy has been conspicuously absent from current literary debate. His novels are seldom marshalled in the interests of narratology, nor do his poems feature in discussions of language and modernity. A cursory check of the indices of advanced literary studies would suggest that Hardy is not a point of reference, a useful instance. Too simple to be interesting, perhaps, too well-liked to be bad, Hardy is the object of a discreet, polite silence.

The only component of the modern critical scene to give sustained attention to Hardy is, surprisingly, feminism. Hardy does not in his fiction avoid stereotyping, and in his personal life he was no exemplary male. Yet in the past 15 years feminists have written much on Hardy, almost always sympathetic. Allied with psychoanalysis, feminism has begun to investigate some of the latent, hitherto invisible, patterns in Hardy's fictions. And it seems to be in the wake of feminism that other contemporary literary students are turning to Hardy, to find what New Criticism both failed to discern and has so far obscured to those who have come after. The complexity of Hardy will soon be cliché. What that complexity means, how it can be analysed or even resolved, are concerns that will feature increasingly in works on Hardy; they take us not beyond this book's scope, but beyond its deadline.

1

Hardy and the Nature of Fiction

Two stories are entrenched: that Hardy was driven to fiction only because he could not find a publisher for his poetry; and that he was extremely sensitive to reviewers and critics. Hardy's own autobiography, 'ghosted' under the name of his widow (see F.E. Hardy, 1962), is a wondrously unsatisfactory read, not just because of the deception that went into its making: that has its intriguing humour. It could not have been published as an autobiography because it contains nothing that is characteristic of the autobiographies of great writers. And by 'great writers' is meant poets and dramatists, not novelists. Wordsworth's *Prelude* is exemplary in English: its subtitle 'Growth of a Poet's Mind', declares the one fit subject. What does not contribute to that growth is mere circumstance, unredeemable contingency. Akin to the *Bildungsroman* of German Romanticism – the novel of development firmly directed towards a clear, high destiny – the poet's autobiography can be inscribed as poetry, or described in prose: Goethe's long *Dichtung und Wahrheit* brings the poet Goethe to the age of twenty-five. In *The Life of the Poet*, a wide-ranging study of the way in which poets shape their lives and perceptions of those lives, Lawrence Lipking (1981) makes the claim that 'every major Western poet after Homer...has left some work that records the principles of his own poetic development...' (p. vii). The nature of Western poetry seems to require such exposure, such self-reference.

It is almost inevitable that Hardy should have no place, no

mention, in Lipking's survey. From Hardy's insistent testimony after 1896 when, following the reviews of *Jude the Obscure*, he abandoned fiction, we assume that he had always wanted to be a poet, and that he wished to be judged by the poetry that he was publishing from 1898 onwards, rather than by his novels. However devious Hardy might have been in his private as well as public utterances, there is no reason to suspect the truth of this. Hardy was writing poetry in the 1860s, and it was not published. Hardy had the sense of a poet's destiny without the means. His autobiography is the obverse of *The Prelude*, for it tells of everything that got in the way. Not just financial need, crass reviewers, difficulties with copyright laws, but *The Return of the Native*, *The Mayor of Casterbridge* and *Tess of the d'Urbervilles*, the great novels themselves, all are obstacles to the poet's progress.

The contradiction is manifest. If he were writing fiction only to make a living, Hardy should not have been so upset by the poor reviews and the lack of critical appreciation. Notoriety always increases sales. One of the anecdotes that has established Hardy's sensitivity to opinion is to be found in *The Early Life of Thomas Hardy 1840-1891*. His first novel *Desperate Remedies*, was reviewed, not kindly, in the *Spectator*:

> He remembered, for long years after, how he had read this review as he sat on a stile leading to the eweleaze he had to cross on his way home to Bockhampton. The bitterness of that moment was never forgotten; at the time he wished that he were dead.

> (F.E. Hardy, 1962, p. 84)

It may come as a surprise that this, one of the best-known passages from the 'Autobiography,' was *not* written by Hardy; it was inserted by his widow Florence Emily Hardy, and J.M. Barrie, her assistant, after Hardy's death. Theirs is the conventional life of the great writer: the poet, lofty, inspired, destined, sits 'on a stile leading to the eweleaze' like a pastoral swain, and is rudely interrupted by the world's rough doings. Clearly he spoke of the episode to Florence – for she would not presume on pure fabrication – but it was exactly the kind of episode that Hardy wanted to keep out of this autobiography (see Millgate, 1984, p. 504).

And, of course, that particular passage is well known precisely because it satisfies *our* expectations; after all, we only read Hardy's autobiography because we acknowledge him as a great writer. But our conventions – unlike those of Hardy's youth – include novelists among 'great writers'. We are heir to the achievements, on behalf of the prestige of all serious novelists, of Flaubert, Henry James, and James Joyce. Hardy never explicitly challenged the mid-Victorian assumption that novelists were entertainers, able to command immense popular esteem but inevitably to be excluded from proper literary greatness. Dickens was, during his lifetime, simply not measured against Tennyson or Browning. The best that one could, as a novelist, hope to achieve was some form of social and ethical improvement. As Hardy wrote in 'The Profitable Reading of Fiction', 'Our true object is a lesson in life, mental enlargement...'. In 1890, by way of a manifesto in advance of the publication of *Tess*, Hardy appealed for 'Candour in English Fiction':

> ...the position of man and woman in nature, and the position of belief in the minds of man and woman – things which everybody is thinking but nobody is saying – might be taken up and treated frankly.
>
> (Orel, 1966, p. 133)

Measured on some hypothetical scale of social and even psychological improvement, Hardy's novels presumably had a beneficial effect: certainly Havelock Ellis, John Addington Symonds, and D.H. Lawrence – to name only the most prominent – acknowledged Hardy's part in the breaking down of Victorian taboos.

Social reformers, however, make no claim to immortality. For the great writer, any social or political consequence of what is written must be incidental. There is a curious, revealing ambiguity in one of Hardy's last letters. Still insisting on the standard version, since 1896, of the poet's postponed destiny, Hardy writes in October 1926:

> Well, as to what I told him of my instinct having been originally towards verse than novel writing, I was correct in saying so, whatever good results may have come from my being forced to take to prose.

> (Purdy and Millgate, 1978-88, vii, p. 46)

'Good results' may be aesthetic – the great novels – or they may be the social consequences of those novels. If the former, this would be almost the only instance of Hardy admitting to pride in his novels; if the latter, Hardy would be remaining faithful to his insistence that it is only the poetry that matters. It now transpires that caution and scepticism should hedge the one well-known instance of Hardy's expression of self-satisfaction on reading through his novels for the Wessex Edition (1911-12):

> I got to like the character of Clym before I had done with him. I think he is the nicest of my heroes, and *not a bit* like me. On taking up *The Woodlanders* and reading it after many years, I think I like it, *as a story*, the best of all....

> (Millgate, 1984, p. 520)

We now learn that Hardy never wrote that in 'a letter to a friend' in 1912, and that the entire passage was added to *The Later Years* only after Hardy's death. The source of this passage may be nowhere but in a general desire to witness Hardy expressing some or any satisfaction in his fiction.

Hardy's insistence on the unimportance of his fiction is to be found from about 1896 onwards, whenever it was that Hardy decided never to write another novel. It is not to be found in writings published before that date. Indeed, the two important essays, 'The Profitable Reading of Fiction' and

'Candour in English Fiction' (1888 and 1890 respectively; see Orel, 1966) attempt to relate ethical and aesthetic concerns: English novels lack candour because they lack form. In the 1888 essay we read:

> Good fiction may be defined here as that kind of imaginative writing which lies nearest to the epic, dramatic, or narrative masterpieces of the past....
>
> Closely connected with the humanizing education found in fictitious narrative which reaches to the level of an illuminant of life, is the aesthetic training....
>
> ...to a masterpiece in story there appertains a beauty of shape, no less than to a masterpiece in pictorial or plastic art.
>
> (Orel, 1966, pp. 114, 120)

This is probably the greatest claim that Hardy makes publicly for the aesthetic possibilities of fiction. It can be no coincidence that the essay was written four years after Henry James' 'The Art of Fiction', which was collected and published in book form in 1888. There James wrote:

> Only a short time ago it might have been supposed that the English novel was not what the French call *disputable*. It had no air of having a theory, a conviction, a consciousness of itself behind it – of being the expression of artistic faith....
>
> (James, 1984, p. 44)

But Hardy, in his essay of 1890, has abandoned the notion that narrative might have 'beauty of shape,' and now rests everything on a vague notion of 'proportion' in the reader's mind:

> Anyhow, conscientious fiction alone it is which can excite a reflective and abiding interest in the minds of thoughtful readers of a mature age, who are weary of puerile inventions and famishing for accuracy; who consider that, in representations of the world, the passions ought to be proportioned

as in the world itself. This is the interest which was excited in the minds of the Athenians by their immortal tragedies, and in the minds of Londoners at the first performance of the finer plays of three hundred years ago. They reflected life, revealed life, criticised life.

(Orel, 1966, p. 127)

The proportion of the passions represented to the mind makes for a most attenuated aesthetics.

What remains consistent throughout these two essays is the sense of drama, specifically tragic drama, as the model for serious fiction. The major shift is from the claim that drama gains its effect through *aesthetic* form, to the claim that drama works through the *mind* of the spectator. The first claim comes as no surprise to the reader of *The Return of the Native*, a novel constructed on dramatic principles, with its five books in place of five acts, its unities of space and time. But with Hardy's last four major novels, *The Mayor of Casterbridge*, *The Woodlanders*, *Tess* and *Jude*, we see a clear development from a shaped story, a story organized in accord with the demands of aesthetic form, to a story fluid in itself, shaped within the reader's mind: a story that has designs on the reader.

During Hardy's years as a novelist critics frequently compared him with Meredith – Meredith being the master of intelligence, sophistication and ambition in fiction. Nowadays few people read Meredith, and it is to Henry James, more exactly Hardy's contemporary, that critics are likely to turn in search of a standard. Hardy himself did precisely that, in reacting to Henry James' scathing review of *Far from the Madding Crowd* (1874). Describing one passage as 'an excellent example of the cleverness which is only cleverness', James went on to object to the novel's length and shapelessness:

Mr Hardy's novel is very long, but his subject is very short and simple, and the work has been distended to its rather formidable dimensions by the infusion of a large amount of

conversational and descriptive padding and the use of an
ingeniously verbose and redundant style. It is inordinately
diffuse, and, as a piece of narrative, singularly inartistic. The
author has little sense of proportion, and almost none of
composition.

(James, 1984, p. 1045)

In 1874 James had published no novel in volume form, for
Watch and Ward (1871) had been serialized only. Then in
astonishing sequence between 1876 and 1881, James
brought out *Roderick Hudson, The American, The Euro-
peans, Washington Square* and *The Portrait of a Lady.* James'
aesthetic intentions had been stated in that same review in
which Hardy was so unjustly attacked:

> ...we confess that we are nevertheless being rapidly urged to
> a conviction that...the day has come round again for some of
> the antique restrictions as to literary form. The three unities,
> in Aristotle's day, were inexorably imposed on Greek tragedy:
> why shouldn't we have something of the same sort for English
> fiction in the day of Mr Hardy?

This is not only the promise of *The Portrait of a Lady* (1881)
but the provocation of *The Return of the Native* (1878). (See
also Millgate, 1971, p. 354.)

Hardy never speaks very warmly of James, but what is
more remarkable is his refusal to be intimidated. When in
the *Life* he tells of the Rabelais Club, founded as 'a declara-
tion for virility in literature', to which Hardy was elected, he
cannot resist adding:

> ...while, it might be added, Henry James, after a discussion,
> was rejected for the lack of that quality, though he was
> afterwards invited as a guest.

(F.E. Hardy, 1962, p. 136)

Seven years later, in 1886, Hardy attended a Rabelais Club

dinner and found himself placed near Henry James,

> who has a ponderously warm manner of saying nothing in
> infinite sentences; and who left suddenly in the midst of the
> meal because he was placed low down the table, as I was.
> Rather comical in Henry.

(Millgate, 1984, p. 187; mostly omitted from
F. E. Hardy, 1962, p. 181)

In the *Life* Hardy relishes the setting down of what James
and Robert Louis Stevenson had to say about *Tess* in 1892,
in some letters which Hardy read when they were published
after James' death:

> Hardy's good-natured friends Henry James and R.L. Steven-
> son (whom he afterwards called the Polonius and the Osric of
> novelists) corresponded about [*Tess*] in this way: 'Oh, yes,
> dear Louis: Tess of the d'Urbervilles is vile. The pretence of
> sexuality is only equalled by the absence of it, [?] and the
> abomination of the language by the author's reputation for
> style.' (*Letters of Henry James.*) When Hardy read this after
> James's death he said, 'How indecent of those two virtuous
> females to expose their mental nakedness in such a manner.'

(Millgate, 1984, p. 259)

Such condescension on Hardy's part seems almost out-
rageous to those readers of fiction for whom James is the
pre-eminent novelist of the language. And for a large number
of critics and teachers of fiction, those in need of 'a theory, a
conviction', the sheer authority of James has been unassail-
able.

It is often assumed that Hardy's hostility to James is that
of a novelist whose methods and aims were entirely different,
as if Hardy had wanted to write (in James' phrase for Tolstoy
and Dostoevsky) 'loose baggy monsters', as if what James saw
as the defects of *Far from the Madding Crowd* were in
Hardy's eyes intended and achieved, to be striven for again

and again in subsequent novels. Hardy responded to James' criticism of 1874, and he continued to respond to it. James may have rankled, but Hardy knew that his recommendations could not be ignored. Both wanted the same thing – for the novel to have the status of great literature – and both had the uneasy knowledge that their enterprise was shared, that in the event of success, each would deserve credit. It was only after the publication of *Jude* that Hardy began publicly to disparage his own novels, and, implicitly, the potential of narrative fiction itself. In his new belated status of poet, Hardy can, in 1903, afford supreme arrogance, in a private letter:

> In my enforced idleness I have been reading H. James's 'Wings of the Dove'– the first of his that I have looked into for years & years. I read it with a fair amount of care – as much as one would wish to expend on any novel, certainly, seeing what there is to read besides novels – and so did Em; but we have been arguing ever since about what happened to the people & find we have wholly conflicting opinions thereon. At the same time James is almost the only living novelist I can read, & taken in small doses I like him exceedingly, being as he is a real man of letters.

> (Purdy and Millgate, 1978-88, iii, p. 56)

The quality of retaliation here is evident only to someone who remembers – as Hardy plainly did – the review of 40 years before, in which this was one of James' strictures:

> If novels were the only books written, novels written on this scale would be all very well; but as they compete, in the esteem of sensible people, with a great many other books, and a great many other objects of interest of all kinds, we are inclined to think that, in the long run, they will be defeated in the struggle for existence unless they lighten their baggage very considerably and do battle in a more scientific equipment.

> (James, 1984, p. 1046)

Hardy took to heart that lesson in economy, and wrote often, as in the already cited letter of 1926, that 'I still feel that I have in many cases concentrated into a page or two of verse what in the novels filled scores of pages'. In economic terms, James' betrayal was immense: in public, after 1894, James penned barely another word about Hardy. Theirs was an extraordinary relationship, or absence of one. Extended over so many years, it may be less poignant but no less symptomatic than the one brief, empty meeting of the two great novelists of the next generation, Proust and Joyce. Geniuses are never so uneasy with each other as when there is almost nothing on which to differ.

The parallel careers of James and Hardy have been sketched here for a number of reasons. By dissolving their apparent and published differences one can understand that they had a common purpose. Both writers are now recognized as great novelists, and both are responsible for the strength and confidence of the novel in the 20th century. Another reason is to show that writers do not derive their inspiration from the void, that Hardy's sensitivity to criticism is fundamentally a readiness to learn and to improve: serious criticism was taken seriously. And the third reason is to show that Hardy's playing down of the merits and importance of his novels was an extended indulgence of *ressentiment*.

As many noted, Max Beerbohm among them, Hardy's was never a convincing pose. Beerbohm's *Sequelula to The Dynasts* is a parody of that most easily parodied of works. But parody is a form of flattery, and within the *Sequelula* Beerbohm ridicules not *The Dynasts* but Hardy's reasons for not writing more novels:

Recording Angel:

Hardy. Mr Thomas.
Novelist. Author of The Woodlanders, Far from the Madding Crowd, The Trumpet-Major,
Tess of the D'Urbervilles, etcetera,
Etcetera. In 1895
Jude the Obscure was published, and a few

Hasty reviewers, having to supply
A column for the day of publication
Filled out their space by saying that there were
Several passages that might have been
Omitted with advantage. Mr. Hardy
Saw that if that was so, well then, of course,
Obviously the only thing to do
Was to write no more novels, and forthwith
Applied himself to Drama, and to Us....

(Cited in Brennecke, 1925, p. 191)

Beerbohm took great care to let it be known that he understood Hardy to be making an excuse so ridiculous that it was
not meant to be taken seriously:

To accept that explanation were to insult him. A puny engine
of art may be derailed by such puny obstacles as the public
can set in its way. So strong an engine as Mr Hardy rushes
straight on, despite them.... Mr Hardy writes no more novels
because he has no more novels to write.

More speculatively we can suppose that by 1896 Hardy was
receiving a very considerable annual income from his novels,
and could now afford to devote his time entirely to poetry
(Millgate, 1982, p. 374, takes this hypothesis for fact). However, it is possible that a further calculation entered into the
decision: if the novel as a form were ever to have stature, then
what Hardy had written so far would probably suffice; but if
great literature continued to be the monopoly of poetry and
drama, then Hardy in 1896 would have very feeble claims. It
may have been some such canny deliberation whose outcome
made Hardy unique in English Literature: one of its greatest
novelists, one of its greatest poets. That verdict was already
being pronounced – with more gesture than conviction – in
the obituaries of 1928, and is today secure, in the curriculum
and in the marketplace.

The explanation that Hardy found it necessary to give, and
repeatedly, for 30 years, for his ceasing to write fiction was

phrased in terms of abandonment and good riddance. As he aged to witness the success of the Jamesian cause, and saw the credit going largely to Henry James, Hardy might have regretted his abandonment of the same cause. His attempts at dissociation were always half-hearted, or equivocal. He could be disparaging about Zola, with whose programme of 'naturalism' Hardy's name was often linked by reviewers; and yet he seems to have avoided Flaubert and Turgenev, the two foreign novelists with similar ambitions for the art of fiction. There is, in fact, no evidence of Hardy's having read *Madame Bovary* or anything else by Flaubert (see Millgate, 1971, pp. 355-7). When in 1899 he was asked to contribute to a symposium on 'Which French authors now dead best represented in their works the distinctive genius of France?', Hardy answered briefly, but showed the breadth of his reading in French literature. His one paragraph contains the names of twenty-six French authors, and although Zola was not yet dead, there is no such easy excuse for his omission of the names of Flaubert, Maupassant or Stendhal (Orel, 1966, p. 140). Hardy's opinion of French novelists might signify too much of the roots and alignments of his own fiction. James knew that he had to labour, through criticism, to create the tradition in which he would have an honoured place; but Hardy would not want to be found taking his own novels so seriously. His complaints about the lack of candour in English fiction are in fact compromised by his lack of concern for Zola and the fate of Zola's translators and publishers. To a friend in 1897 Hardy wrote: 'You mistake in supposing I admire Zola. It is just what I don't do' (Purdy and Millgate, 1978-88, ii, p. 157).

Hardy made himself, as a novelist, hard to place within any tradition or tendency, and the consequence is that while his greatness is recognized, his place in the history of fiction and, especially, in the history of the theory of fiction, is uncertain. This explains why there is such an enormous body of criticism devoted to Hardy, and why Hardy figures so slightly in more general or theoretical studies of fiction.

One would especially like to know Hardy's response to one of the most sophisticated books of criticism devoted to his

novels to be published during his own lifetime. *The Technique
of Thomas Hardy* by Joseph Warren Beach, professor of
English at the University of Minnesota, appeared in 1922,
after Beach had published studies of Meredith and James.
His book on Hardy was published just months after Percy
Lubbock's *The Craft of Fiction*, the critical work that initiated
(under the aegis of James) the study of the theory of narrative
in the English-speaking world. We read in Beach's Preface:

> Studies in the technique of the novel are, it seems to me,
> unduly rare. The literary history of the novel has been largely
> taken up with subject-matter, style, social significance, the
> differentiae of realism and romanticism. Until the appear-
> ance a few months ago of Mr. Percy Lubbock's brilliant and
> subtle book on *The Craft of Fiction*, the novel has been very
> little subjected to that technical study which has been carried
> so far with the epic, the sonnet, the short story, the drama.
> By technique I mean the structural art of the novel: the
> method of assembling and ordering these elements of subject-
> matter, social criticism, and the like. The novel has been so
> democratic a medium, so little regarded as anything more
> than an evening's entertainment or the vehicle of instruction
> and propaganda, that scant attention has been given, espe-
> cially in Saxon countries, to strictly artistic standards ap-
> plying to it....
>
> It is not by accident that the author of *The Craft of Fiction*
> is one who was a personal friend of Henry James and the
> editor of his letters [the volumes wherein Hardy had read of
> James's opinion of *Tess*]. No writer of novels in English has
> given more attention than James to the question of technique,
> and probably none has had a stronger influence on the tech-
> nique of novelists now writing....
>
> (Beach, 1922, p. v-vi)

We might, after this, expect Hardy to be the victim of a
hatchet-job. Instead, through a measured disclaimer of certainty and a re-definition of technique, we discover:

In the case of Hardy, the reader must often wonder whether he was a deliberate structural artist, whether the occasional greatness of his work was not rather the result of a technique which came to him, as we say, by inspiration, and whether indeed the unfailing charm of his work, in whatever degree of greatness, is not something independent of questions of technique. Technique is but one of several factors determining the appeal of any writer; and Hardy with his frequent obliviousness to art is a greater novelist than James with his unceasing vigilance.

(Beach, 1922, p. viii)

To acknowledge such praise would be for Hardy to compromise all that he had said about his novels in the previous 25 years, and to put at risk the dawning recognition of his poetry. Of the fifteen or so full-length critical (not topographical) books devoted to Hardy and published before his death, this is the only one about which Hardy makes no comment whatever. (He does not comment, either, on *Thomas Hardy from Serial to Novel* by Beach's student Mary Ellen Chase, but as this was published within months of Hardy's death it is unlikely that he read it; Beach's book, however, was in Hardy's study of Max Gate.)

Beach's enterprise, as seen in 1922, appears to be founded on paradox and near-contradiction. Lubbock's principles are designed to enable one to distinguish technical accomplishment, to see the superiority of James, to recognize what Hardy lacks. Beach accepts this, but goes on to claim that Hardy is the greater novelist in spite of his paying less attention to technique. Technique cannot then mean what Beach first said it meant, 'the structural art of the novel'. Rather than argue his case in theoretical terms – and Bakhtin alone has offered a serious theoretical defence of the 'loose, baggy monster' – Beach makes a historical argument. He opens his case with a plea for selection, and already by 1922 his was a familiar observation: 'The most remarkable thing about Mr. Hardy's novels, for anyone who takes them in sequence, is their extreme unevenness of quality' (Beach, 1922, p. 3).

The first two book-length studies of Hardy, by Lionel Johnson and Annie Macdonell, were both published in 1894, and – even before the publication of *Jude* and the announced completion of Hardy's work as a novelist – there is already an absolutely clear consensus. For Lionel Johnson (1894) there are six great novels, *A Pair of Blue Eyes, Far from the Madding Crowd, The Return of the Native, The Mayor of Casterbridge, The Woodlanders* and *Tess*. The prominence of *A Pair of Blue Eyes* is the only oddity to us, almost a century later: it appealed enormously to Tennyson, Patmore and other high and eminent Victorians (contrast F. E. Hardy, 1962, pp. 104-5 with Millgate, 1984, pp. 107-8). Annie Macdonnell, in her book of 1894, claims greatness for five novels, ranking *The Woodlanders* just below them: *Far from the Madding Crowd, The Return of the Native, The Trumpet-Major, The Mayor* and *Tess*. Few would place *The Trumpet-Major* above *The Woodlanders*, but hardly any would want to exclude it, or *Under the Greenwood Tree*, from any list of favourite Hardy novels. Of the fourteen novels there has been a lasting consensus about the six great ones (*Far from the Madding Crowd, Return of the Native, The Mayor of Caster-bridge, The Woodlanders, Tess of the d'Urbervilles* and *Jude the Obscure*), the two idyllic ones (*Under the Greenwood Tree, The Trumpet-Major*), and the six relative failures (*Desperate Remedies, A Pair of Blue Eyes, The Hand of Ethelberta, A Laodicean, Two on a Tower* and *The Well-Beloved*). The disturbing feature is not that an author should write some good and some less good books, but that Hardy had them alternating through the 25 years of his novel-writing career. *Far from the Madding Crowd*, considered by a number of both early and recent critics to be the best of all, was Hardy's fourth novel, and *The Well-Beloved* was written between *Tess* and *Jude*.

One other difference in evaluation between 1894 and the present concerns the status of Hardy's short stories. Then – following Hardy's own example in the Wessex Edition – they were included in all processes of measurement, classification and evaluation; throughout most of the 20th century Hardy's short stories have been relegated to separate treatment, and are not even mentioned in some of the studies that claim to offer a survey of all Hardy's work. There are more dutiful chapters on *The Dynasts* than on the short stories. And until 1988 there was no complete edition of the short stories available in paperback.

Beach is himself dismissive of the short stories, regarding them merely as occasions for Hardy to exploit his fascination with local history: 'that devoted antiquarianism of the hermit of Dorchester which he has indulged in many of the short stories' (Beach, 1922, p. 113). That exclusion aside, however, Beach is prepared to account for all the novels, to confront the mockery of progress that we find in the sequence: *Far from the Madding Crowd* (1874), *The Hand of Ethelberta* (1876), *The Return of the Native* (1878), *The Trumpet-Major* (1880), *A Laodicean* (1881), *Two on a Tower* (1882), and *The Romantic Adventures of a Milkmaid* (1883). To this latter, by far the most justly neglected of all Hardy's fictions, Beach devotes three pages:"there is something brazen in coming to us, the connoisseurs, with such wares' (Beach, 1922, p. 4). Even though Beach suspects that Hardy intended *The Romantic Adventures* merely as a potboiler for commercial success, he is not willing to ignore the offence. For Beach, Hardy's 'relapses' are instructive.

Hardy's pictorialism had been noted very early. Indeed, such recognition had been elicited by the subtitle of *Under the Greenwood Tree*: 'A Rural Painting of the Dutch School'. By 1894 Annie Macdonnell could claim that Hardy 'comes nearer to having the vision and using the methods of a painter than any other novelist' (Macdonell, 1894, p. 16). Beach regards this pictorialism as a constant danger for Hardy. Although Beach is not explicit, it is presumably related to Hardy's antiquarianism: both avail themselves of perspective, but perspective can be used not for cognition and ordering, but for wilful distancing and merely decorative sentiment. (For a thorough treatment of pictorialism and related aspects of Hardy's fiction, see Bullen, 1986.)

The advance of *Far from the Madding Crowd* over *Under the Greenwood Tree* is, for Beach, to be located in the mingling of plot and picture, each restraining the other:

It is a question whether Gabriel or Bathsheba should be regarded as the leading character. As Bathsheba is undoubtedly the central actor in the drama, so Oak is the central feature of the pictorial composition.

(Beach, 1922, p. 53)

This is a shrewd observation, for it enables us to see the union of Bathsheba and Gabriel not as the dynamic convergence of two movements but as Bathsheba's coming to rest in that which has never moved. For Beach the novel's triumph is due to its setting, and it works because Oak expresses the setting, is part of it, not a character acting in front of it. It is the absence of such an integrated figure in some of Hardy's other novels that reduces setting to background, ornamentation in the long perspective. Beach sees *The Return of the Native* as a further advance:

This is the first of the novels...to exhibit in striking fashion that tendency to dramatic structure which is so generally prominent in the novels of today, and which has been coming into fashion since about the time of its conception.

(Beach, 1922, p. 80)

Beach, himself author of previous studies of Meredith and James, is keen to emphasize Hardy's priority, suggesting that his influence on Meredith and James has been obscured by their adoption of a comic mode in response to Hardy's tragic drama. In 1877, says Beach, 'Meredith delivered his famous lecture on comedy' (Beach, 1922, p. 88), and in 1879, the year after *The Return*, he published *The Egoist*. To Hardy is credited the introduction into the novel of design, dramatic principles, the unities, and the subservience of narration to dialogue – of what James would later term 'telling' to 'showing'.

What the novel must dispense with is, then, the inessential and extraneous, the difference, for Beach, between 'subject' and 'theme': 'In his early novels we might say that Mr Hardy was treating a subject, but not a theme' (Beach, 1922, p. 90).

This could be an important distinction, especially if we consider what happens to the 'content' of the novel between, say, Dickens and James, but more specification is needed if we are to appreciate Hardy's part in that transformation. Beach implies that James' novels 'following *The Spoils of Poynton*, such as *The Awkward Age* and *The Ambassadors*' (Beach, 1922, p. 89), can trace their lineage through Meredith to *The Return of the Native*. Of the dialogue between the dying Mrs Yeobright and Johnny Nunsuch Beach writes:

> There are few places in which Hardy – few places in which any English novelist – has made himself so completely free from the commonplace bustle of the theater, and has made us hear so pure and unstrained the voices of the inner drama.

> (Beach, 1922, p. 93)

That challenge by parenthesis might prompt Beach's reader to propose Isabel Archer thinking into the night: *The Portrait of a Lady* was published three years later, in 1881.

However convincing or otherwise one might find Beach's argument – and it has been ignored rather than refuted – it was exceptional at that time, and for many years subsequently, to treat Hardy formally instead of 'philosophically'. Hardy was much too gloomy to be comparable to James. If critics noted the dramatic structure they would put the emphasis on the 'tragic' rather than the 'dramatic'. For Beach, however, the mood of *The Return* is subordinate to the means of its expression:

> It is only once or twice in Meredith, and more generally in the later novels of James, that we find so great a volume of emotional energy released by events of so little objective importance. Only in them is found a greater economy of incident; and many more readers will testify to the dramatic intensity of *The Native* than to that of *The Egoist* or *The Golden Bowl*.

> (Beach, 1922, pp. 93-4)

'Dramatic economy' is achieved through the unities of place and time. To stick to a single location is an obvious way of transforming background into setting, and subject into theme. Likewise, the unity of time compresses the action, and makes clear what is and is not essential. For Beach, *The Return of the Native* has introduced into the English novel the dramatic unities of time and place, but Hardy himself was not to repeat his achievement.

While Meredith and James, according to Beach, were developing the possibilities opened up by *The Return*, Hardy was moving on, even if this involved 'certain backward tendencies in novelistic art' (Beach, 1922, p. 110). In order to remain Hardy's advocate Beach argues for deliberate regression:

> *The Mayor of Casterbridge* and *The Woodlanders*...are both books in which it is hard to distinguish more than the most rudimentary acquaintance with that art in the narrative of events which was at the disposal of any well-read novelist in the years 1886 and 1887. There is only one alternative to this conclusion: that the author may in both cases have deliberately chosen, as proper to his subject or congenial to his readers, a technique of slapdash facility and looseness.... *The Mayor of Casterbridge* departs even farther than *The Woodlanders* from the method of sober and shapely drama, reminding one often of the moving picture, which has flourished so remarkably during the generation following its appearance.
>
> (Beach, 1922, p. 134)

'Movie' is a word first coined in 1913; less than 10 years later it was used as the title of Beach's chapter on *The Mayor of Casterbridge*. Hardy's anticipations of the cinema have been remarked upon by later commentators such as David Lodge (Lodge, 1973-4) and, with specific reference to *The Dynasts*, by John Wain (Wain, 1965, pp. ix-x; see also Grundy, 1979, ch. 4). The rapid shifts of viewpoint, focus, angle and perspective that characterize *The Dynasts* and are present in all Hardy's writings make the cinematic analogy almost inevitable. But is it of more significance than an analogy between Tennyson's famously myopic observations and the zoom lens? Beach's point is less random, and more subtle.

'Drama' and 'economy' are Beach's touchstones, and when economy is lacking Hardy is compared to the Prodigal Son:

> Of such economy Mr. Hardy had shown more than a notion in *A Pair of Blue Eyes* and *The Native*, as he was destined to show it again in *Tess* and *Jude*. But in *The Mayor of Caster-bridge* he wastes his substance in the most riotous fashion.

> (Beach, 1922, p. 146)

Beach shows how psychological tautness and inwardness, 'the intimate significance, the sense of being on the inside', are simply not present where they ought to be, and where we expect them to be: 'But Hardy is concerned with nothing further, on the side of art, than the *irony* involved...' (Beach, 1922, p. 147). 'Nothing further than the *irony*': that phrase, with its italicized disdain, might have forestalled the critical (New Critical) short-changing that would accept irony as sufficient, as an aesthetic virtue. Although irony needs a degree of inwardness, of psychological consciousness, in order to set up the imbalance of knowledge on which its effects depend, there is a necessary subordination: the intimate processes of the consciousness are, in Hardy at least, subordinated to the external presentation of an ironic scene. Beach assumes the prosecutor's laconic mode:

> It is true that we have here some half-dozen pictures admirably adapted to the screen.
> And something of the sort may be said for the book as a whole. There is matter here for half a dozen novels; but what is given is hardly more than the scenario of a movie.

> (Beach, 1922, p. 147)

But that is not the final verdict:

The miracle of *The Mayor of Casterbridge* is that, with such a staggering burden of overhead expenses in the way of mere plot, the author can still pay dividends on the income from character.

(Beach, 1922, p. 234)

Henchard is dramatically, visibly, physically present to the reader precisely because his own consciousness, his inner life, is so unsubtle, finding expression not in interior debate and reasoning but only in action. Beach hints at the exclusiveness of the Jamesian novel: its characters have to be extraordinarily subtle in thought and speech. There is little evidence, but we might speculate that Henchard represents Hardy's deliberate intention to avoid that particular temptation. Hardy's interest in and sympathy with uneducated people, those whose lack of sophistication does nothing to advance an author's claim thereto, has of course attracted the approving interest of critics with politically progressive leanings.

Michel Foucault has made fashionable the notion that the only power is power over discourse, that language is an instrument of oppression, its victims the inarticulate, the speechless, the dumb. Beach's understanding of Henchard is extremely pertinent when we recall that in 1922 his use of the word 'movie' connotes and presupposes 'silent':

And if Michael Henchard is a convincing and appealing figure, he is one well cast for his part in a story that is so like a moving-picture film. He is, after all, beneath his civil garb and chain of office, the original caveman, ever readier with blows than words.... In a world of talk, he is almost inarticulate.

(Beach, 1922, p. 154)

Any book, any text, is a 'world of talk', and that world is inhospitable to the inarticulate, like Henchard, and to those, like Jude, whose articulation is outside the official discourse.

Beach's study is symptomatic of a deep conflict. On the one

hand we admire James for his 'mastery' of discourse at its most sophisticated and implicated, and for his represent-ation of the discourses of others, themselves hardly less sophisticated than their author's; we admire the aesthetic coherence and consistency which hold dialogue, internal monologue and diegesis and description on a single plane. On the other hand we may find the representation of discourses to be achieved at the expense of the representation of char-acters as physical beings in a physical world, a world not of talk but of things. In an essay of 1960 in *The Charted Mirror*, 'Tess of the d'Urbervilles and The Awkward Age', John Hol-loway takes Hardy as the apt contrast to James:

> Here, Hardy's novel seems to me much the greater. Tess the individual human, Tess as part of a social texture, Tess as ultimately an animal with an animal's task of maintaining life – Hardy sees all of these, they all enter into his account; but *The Awkward Age* constantly seems to invite awareness of what it then passes over in silence, or even positively excludes.

> (Holloway, 1960, p. 115)

What is excluded is that which is outside discourse, the physical world and the bodies in it that are simply there:

> James's moral insight is communicated at the price of no communication over what the moral insight was insight into; and through a good deal of this novel, he seems to have too full a sense of the issues, the necessary moral discriminations; and too thin a sense of the life, the realities, between which those issues must lie.

> (Holloway, 1960, p. 116)

The easy separation between life and reality on one side and moral insight and discrimination on the other now seems naive: what do we know of 'life' or 'reality' that is not mediated through our own insights and discriminations? But what is not naive, what needs serious elaboration, is Holloway's sense that there is no direct ratio between 'worth' and 'degrees of articulation'. The condition of James' aesthetic achievement is an inescapably circular trap: the more sophisticated the articulation of a moral decision, the better morally it will be.

In a view of Henchard consonant with Beach's idea of the 'caveman', Holloway (in another essay, 'Hardy's Major Fiction') develops Henchard's simile of himself 'as if I were a bull breaking fence:'

> Henchard is not, of course, *simply* an animal. At no point does metaphor become literal truth. But it is through this metaphor that we must see the struggle which constitutes the narrative and the unity of the book....

> (Holloway, 1960, p. 103)

Holloway is concerned with a 'historicist' reading of Hardy, in which the old and valuable is superseded by the new and inferior:

> Henchard is more than slaved, he is *tamed*. That is something more thorough-going. It is the measure of what Hardy sees as at issue. The work of his novel, focused in the metaphor of man and beast, is to depict and narrate the conquest and domestication of one way of life (the traditional way) by another.

> (Holloway, 1960, p. 104)

If we here recall Beach's insight we will understand that one of the most effective ways to tame a man is to teach him to speak, to give up blows for words. Literature and the study of literature take for granted the superiority of words over blows, of pens over swords, even perhaps of words over deeds. And yet in certain texts we find on the part of the author an envy of those outside the dispensation, heroines and heroes whose lives are of such action, actuality and immediacy as to be self-evidently superior to the texts that represent them. Henchard is one, Kazantzakis' Zorba another; likewise this envy threatens to disrupt anything written by D.H. Lawrence or Hemingway – their texts vitiated just because they are *written*.

Identification with characters is one of the simpler pleasures of reading Hardy, but not, I think, of reading James. Identification provides us with a vicarious experience, and doubly so: we are not there because we are here with a text, and we are subject, in most of Hardy's novels from *Under the Greenwood Tree*, to a temporal lapse. The stories are set in a past that is gone, and Hardy's Wordsworthian sense of loss and regret is almost necessarily conveyed to the reader. As an instance of academic criticism at its most desperate, we might note Virginia Hyman's *Ethical Perspective in the Novels of Thomas Hardy* (1975), whose thesis is that readers may prefer the old order to the new, but that Hardy does not:

> Hardy shows Henchard increasingly as belonging to an older order and as acting upon impulses that are essentially self-destructive. Over against Henchard's values he sketches in his own, in the characterizations of Farfrae and Elizabeth Jane.
>
> (Hyman, 1975, p. 6)

That is the sort of thing that anyone might maintain for as long as it takes to get a Ph.D., and much of the published criticism of Hardy is approximately of this kind. But it is more interesting to suppose – more ingenious, even – that the reader's sympathy for Henchard over Farfrae, for Tess over Angel Clare, is bound up with the act of reading. We do not feel sympathy with those characters of similar educational and intellectual attainment to ourselves, as we do in the novels of George Eliot or James. And by *identifying* with Henchard or Tess the reader is lamenting what might have been had he or she not learnt to read, not been tamed by education.

Identification with characters may not be the noblest aim

of reading, but it is an invitation that the most experienced reader has to resist in Hardy's novels. And because we do not want that resistance to be impoverishing, so we continue to gesture towards the life, the landscape, the characters, the historical context, as if all these had an existence (as Tess herself had for Hardy) independent of the text. Critics of an ideological, historicist, political or otherwise contextualist persuasion seldom apologize for using Hardy's novels as evidence or illustrative material; if not oblivious of the distinction between literature and document, they presume that with Hardy the conflation is acceptable or even necessary: exclude all that, and what is left of Hardy?

The most recent literary criticism, taking its bearings from Barthes, Foucault, Lacan or Derrida, is embarrassed by any notion of *hors texte*: what is not actually written is merely encoded in other semiotic systems. And a reading of Hardy that explained agricultural and rural circumstances in terms of wage contracts and deeds of sale and leaseholds and other documents would be quite acceptable (see Snell, 1985; Barrell, 1982). There are enough contracts and messages and letters and texts (Harmon, 1988) to plot any thesis of the circulation of discourse, and enough missing or undelivered letters to satisfy any appetite for absent signifiers (Hillis Miller, 1984). What is disconcerting about such critical procedures is not that they are different or difficult or foreign but that they have about them a whiff of self-interest. To posit the textuality of all things is a convenience for those academics and intellectuals whose lives are bound to texts – almost a mitigation.

The achievement of, among others, Flaubert, James and Joyce, was to give the novel status as a literary art. The consequence of that achievement has been a sly inversion: fiction has been famously capacious, an all-absorbing, nought-excluding, rag-bag of God's plenty. The 19th century celebrated its powers of self-representation, but rarely thought of novels as literature. Now that novels are studied as literature, that capaciousness has been turned inside out – and text is everywhere, everything is text. Hardy, unlike James or Joyce, is resistant to such reading, which is why contemporary criticism of semiotic or deconstructive tendency neglects the novels, and why feminists, Marxists and historians can make unashamed assumption of the novels' referentiality to a world out there, autonomous, independent of text. Beach's observation, that in a world of talk Henchard is almost inarticulate, provides an explanation. The dumbness of many characters in Hardy's novels, which is extended to the metaphoric field of 'beast' or 'animal,' ensures a stubborn residue of the non-textual. The word 'dumb' should have the pejorative sense, for this is not the silence of cunning or discretion, but the silence of those who, thinking little, have nothing to say. It might be worth noting that this is the single most important aspect of Hardy's influence on Lawrence, who probably even more than Hardy uses beast or animal metaphors for his characters. D.H. Lawrence and Hardy are alike in their critical respectability, their popularity with the general reader, in receiving the attention of feminist and sociological critics, and in their lack of popularity with those critics for whom Joyce and James are touchstones.

We return to the honest perplexity of Joseph Warren Beach in 1922. According to the principles of James, as rendered prescriptive by Percy Lubbock, *The Return of the Native* ought to be Hardy's masterpiece, and all the novels after that a falling off. Beach remains faithful not to the principles but to his own experience as a reader, and is reduced to the embarrassment of evoking the miraculous to explain the disparity between theory and practice:

> The miracle of *The Mayor of Casterbridge* is that, with such a staggering burden of overhead expenses in the way of mere plot, the author can still pay dividends on the income from character.

> (Beach, 1922, p. 234)

The embarrassment is of course compounded by the financial metaphor. A similar disparity is implied by the comment of another early critic, Arthur McDowall, writing in 1931: 'Sometimes one feels that all that is greatest in [Hardy's novels] is not of the essence of the novel' (McDowall, 1931, p. 60). Since James, criticism has been burdened by the knowledge of what a novel is.

The name 'novel' insists not only on novelty but on freedom from prescription. Once a prescriptive theory (or even a set of conflicting theories) has taken over, standards and expectations have to be met. The greatest of novelists, Tolstoy and Dostoevsky, could be charged, by James, with producing 'loose, baggy monsters'. The loose and the baggy must now take form, and conform.

Samuel Chew in *Thomas Hardy: Poet and Novelist*, published in 1921 (the year before Beach's study), considers the possibility that Hardy had intended to set up his own 'theory of the novel', as a rival to other theories and as a justification or explanation of his own novels:

> That he set about the writing of these books [*Tess* and *Jude*] with a full consciousness that they would occasion adverse comment and disturb many minds is shown by the fact that even before *Tess* appeared he published two articles that are in the nature of manifestos.

> (Chew, 1921, p. 57)

Chew refers to 'The Profitable Reading of Fiction' of 1888 and 'Candour in English Fiction' of 1890; he could have strengthened his case by mentioning also 'The Science of Fiction,' published in April 1891. Chew's point is that the last two great novels are not 'characteristic' because they are written according to a theory: this opinion has been voiced by many later critics. Chew would apparently prefer that Hardy had written neither those essays nor those two novels, and yet, as the essays have been written, Chew would like to see them celebrated:

> ...the too little-known essay on 'The Profitable Reading of Fiction', which, if reprinted with authorization, would take its place with Henry James's prefaces and the preface to *The Nigger of the 'Narcissus'*.

> (Chew, 1921, p. 80)

Although these essays have since 1925 been easily available (most conveniently in Orel, 1966) critics of Hardy have usually chosen to ignore them. It is unclear whether this is because the essays seem relatively unimportant, or because Hardy's admirers would prefer to think that the novels were written without a theory in mind.

Virginia Woolf finds herself in contradiction when in her essay 'The Novels of Thomas Hardy' (see Woolf, 1932) she makes a distinction between 'conscious' and 'unconscious' writers. Among the former she cites James and Flaubert, among the latter Dickens, Scott and Hardy. In support of her thesis Woolf quotes not from the essays written, according to Chew, as manifestos, but from the defensive Preface to the Fifth Edition (1892: Orel, 1966) of *Tess*, 'a novel is an impression, not an argument', and from the much later Preface to a volume of verse, *Poems of The Past and The Present* (1901: Orel, 1966):

> Unadjusted impressions have their value, and the road to a true philosophy of life seems to lie in humbly recording diverse readings of its phenomena as they are forced upon us by chance and change.

> (Woolf, 1932, p. 194)

Even while asserting that Hardy 'at his greatest...gives us impressions; at his weakest, arguments', Woolf neglects to mention those more prescriptive essays which would in fact lend support to her contention that *Jude* is 'the most painful' of Hardy's novels: 'In *Jude the Obscure* argument is allowed to dominate impression...' (Woolf, 1932, p. 194).

Hardy, when he is good, is unconscious. When he is bad it is not, for Woolf, because he follows a deliberate, conscious plan, but because he forgets or overlooks his attitude, made defensively and after the fact of writing, of what we might term 'conscious unconsciousness' or 'planned irresponsibility'.

Virginia Woolf's notion of the 'unconscious author' has been influential in approaches to Hardy. The obvious contradictions are not addressed in even the most elaborate and otherwise useful studies of Hardy's 'artless' fictional art, of which Ian Gregor's *The Great Web* (1974) is the most striking example. But the attribution of unconsciousness to Hardy serves the primary function of rescuing Hardy from 'the theory of fiction', even his own theory. And another purpose is served in consequence: to those critics interested in the place of workers in rural society, changes in that society, relationships between classes, the advent of industrial agriculture – to name some of the most frequently treated topics in contextual studies of Hardy – the presumption of unconsciousness is extremely useful. That presumption gives to what Hardy writes a documentary value insofar as it reduces the possibility of distortion through aesthetic shaping or ideological intention.

I had hoped to say almost nothing about a very large number of books on Hardy that constitute the topographical interest. From Wilkinson Sherren's *The Wessex of Romance* and Bertram Windle's *The Wessex of Thomas Hardy*, both published in 1902, to Gordon Beningfield's *The Hardy Country* of 1983 (and into the far future) runs the babbling brook of the Hardy industry. For the legitimate validity of topographical curiosity, there are only two books that matter: *Thomas Hardy's Wessex* (1913) by Hermann Lea – written with Hardy's assistance and approval – and *Hardy's Wessex Re-appraised* (1972) by Denys Kay-Robinson. (For critical use of topography, see Enstice, 1979.) But the very popularity and, more significantly, the plausibility of the topographical approach to Hardy reinforce the notion of the unconscious author who simply records what is there. It is not my intention to suggest that such studies as Merryn Williams' *Thomas Hardy and Rural England* (1972) or the various writings on Hardy by Raymond Williams belong to the picturesque-sentimental line of derivation. But the connection should be made: for all the obsessive fastidiousness of Joyce's 'recreation' of Dublin in 1904, *Ulysses* is not taken for its documentary value, or not at least without much apology and disclaiming; nor do social historians turn to James' novels for documentation of, say, transatlantic travel in 1880.

We could attempt to explain the breadth and multifariousness of Hardy's popularity in terms of a coalition of three groups: those who read the novels for a sense of identification with the characters and for a nostalgic evocation of an England perpetually vanishing; those who use Hardy's novels as documentary evidence of social movements and historical change; and those critics who have little time for novels with theories or theories of the novel. We shall look at some of these latter critics in the next chapter.

There is another approach to Hardy that has generated a great number of studies, but which I propose (consciously) to overlook entirely. This is the philosophical approach, maintained by those who through some unexplained leap of faith believe Hardy to be a great thinker whose literary works are fables for our enlightenment. From Helen Garwood's *Thomas Hardy: An Illustration of the Philosophy of Schopenhauer* (1911), through Herbert Grimsditch's *Character and Environment in the Novels of Thomas Hardy* (1925), Ernest Brennecke's *Thomas Hardy's Universe* (1926), Patrick Braybrooke's *Thomas Hardy and His Philosophy* (1928), and A.P. Elliott's *Fatalism in the Works of Thomas Hardy* (1935) to F.R. Southerington's *Hardy's Vision of Man* (1971) and G.W. Sherman's *The Pessimism of Thomas Hardy* (1976) – to mention only the few that grate on the memory – runs a line of interpreters blissfully, earnestly unconcerned as to whether the text in hand is a novel, a poem, a treatise or a sermon. The interest, again, is solely symptomatic; and probably the only other writer comparably afflicted by such an approach – and then not beyond the mid-20th century – was Browning. But the symptomatic interest is clear: texts can be read as expressions of philosophy only if it can be presumed that no mediation or distortion occurs. And if Hardy has no conscious aesthetic or theoretical intention then it can indeed be supposed that there would be no motive for any such distortion. The corrective, and the appropriate negotiation between 'thoughts' and 'literature', remains the chapter on Hardy in John Holloway's *The Victorian Sage* (1953). (See also ch. 8 of Beer, 1983.)

The topographical, the documentary, the philosophical: all these approaches to a text are made possible by the presumed absence from that text of a conscious theory. The honest and disinterested recognition of Beach, Woolf and others that Hardy is outside the Jamesian tradition of modern fiction has made possible not only the above-mentioned aberrations but also a body of fine, sensitive and distinguished criticism.

2

Multiple Visions:
Early Assessments of Hardy's
Achievement

Thomas Hardy died in 1928. Ten years later W.R. Rutland
began his ambitious *Thomas Hardy: A Study of his Writings
and their Background* with some remarks on the quantity of
secondary literature already available:

> More than fifty publications concerned with Thomas Hardy
> have appeared; but, as far as I know, only one goes beyond
> general discussion, and that one [Ruth Firor, *Folkways in
> Thomas Hardy*, 1931] confines itself to the very special field
> of folklore. This abundance of commentary has absolved me
> from the task of making yet another; for there are now at least
> half a dozen excellent general critical studies of Hardy.
>
> (Rutland, 1938, p. vii)

It is worth pausing over this 'distribution of the secondary'.
Among those 'excellent' general studies Rutland would
presumably have intended to include those of Lionel Johnson
(1894), Annie Macdonnel (1894), Lascelles Abercrombie
(1912), Harold Child (1916), H.C. Duffin (1916), Samuel C.
Chew (1928) and Arthur Macdowall (1931). Rutland omits to
mention the 'philosophical treatment' given to Hardy by such

early studies as those by Helen Garwood (1911), Patrick Braybrooke (1928) and R. E. Zachrisson (1931). Some of these go 'beyond general discussion', but none achieves the dubious distinction of being a work of specialization.

There were, by 1938, several works resulting from serious research, and these Rutland pretends to ignore even while listing them in his bibliography. He does not mention Beach, whose superiority over almost anything written on Hardy until 1940 could be attributed to sophistication of theory rather than to specialization. But there are three books that are clearly graduate theses, of such lasting usefulness that they are still worth consulting: Mary Ellen Chase's *Thomas Hardy: From Serial to Novel* (1927), Elizabeth Cathcart Hickson's *The Versification of Thomas Hardy* (1931) and Ruth Firor's *Folkways in Thomas Hardy* (1931). Chase studied under Beach at the University of Minnesota, and her thesis demonstrates that influence. Firor and Hickson (as well as Helen Garwood) were the students of Cornelius Weygandt at the University of Philadelphia. Firor's comprehensive study has never been superseded, even though she worked in entire ignorance of J. S. Udal's *Dorsetshire Folklore*, first privately printed in 1922. It was not until the 1960s that scholars began serious work on the textual revisions of Hardy's novels, and since then Chase's work has been frequently cited. While many of Chase's claims and conclusions have been invalidated or improved upon with respect to individual novels, her work has been matched only in Simon Gatrell's *Hardy the Creator: A Textual Biography*, published in 1988 (see Gatrell, 1988, p. ix). And the first attempt not just to improve on Hickson's work but simply to take it, and Hardy's prosody, seriously, is Dennis Taylor's *Hardy's Metres and Victorian Prosody*, also published in 1988 (see Taylor, 1988, p. 71).

A number of considerations arise, apart from one's curiosity as to the subsequent careers, if any, of these early Hardy scholars. The works of Chase, Firor and Hickson have all proved themselves useful, and all to some extent justify (to a reader of today, looking back) the specialization of the academic profession. I have already ventured that specialization lends little to our understanding of Hardy; revising this, we might suppose that our understanding of Hardy might have been very different had these studies been taken as exemplary. Instead they were, in the legacy of the gentlemanly tradition of 'English letters', disdained as the efforts of critics thrice-disadvantaged – professional, American, female. And if that was the predictable response it is the more regrettable that their work fared no better with the advent of New Criticism. Thus the tradition of Hardy criticism in the first half of the 20th century – which would serve as foil to the New Criticism – was constituted by those 'excellent general critical studies' (Rutland's phrase) that are unmarked by the sweat of scholarly research.

Before looking at some of the monographs we should note the first attempts in essay form to grasp the shape of Hardy's fiction, as a sequence or as a whole. The earliest of these seems to have been the anonymous essay in *New Quarterly Magazine* of October 1879 which concentrates on *A Pair of Blue Eyes*, *Far from the Madding Crowd* and *Return of the Native*, and which is clearly motivated by alarm that in *The Return* Hardy has taken the wrong direction, has not fulfilled what was promised in the earlier novels:

> At the climax of his dramatic genius, Mr. Hardy has been overtaken by a motive, or by a moral self-consciousness which is equivalent to one...the question stands thus; imagination and intellect are fighting for mastery in Mr. Hardy's work. Which will prevail? Will the unconscious inspiration assimilate the motive? or will the consciousness of the motive paralyse the inspiration?

> (Cox, 1970, p. 70)

The terms are familiar even now: unconscious inspiration has to do battle against a consciousness both of artistry and of dogma. That the writing of great novels should be a peculiar form of sleep-walking is an assumption hardly worthy of contradiction. What matters, and needs elaborating, is the ideological potential of the assumption of unconsciousness:

the critic *knows* Hardy's texts better than their author does, and whatever is unattractive, inconvenient or embarrassing can be lightly dismissed as a somnambulistic stumble.

The *New Quarterly*'s anonymous essayist goes further, by asserting that the greatness of the work is threatened precisely by the consciousness of the author. We love Hardy's novels, but we don't like what Hardy (rather than his novels) is trying to tell us. The obvious critical temptation is to divide the novels into the good and the less good, the boundary being formed by the degree of consciousness at work. *A Laodicean*, *Two on a Tower*, *The Hand of Ethelberta*, *The Well-Beloved* are routinely dismissed for suffering from an excess of authorial consciousness. Curiously, *A Laodicean* is explained away on the grounds provided by Hardy himself, that he had to meet the deadline and fulfil his contract in spite of a debilitating illness. One might have supposed that under the influence of sufficiently soporific medication Hardy would have written his masterpiece.

Notable in this and another anonymous survey in the *British Quarterly Review* is the reasonable assumption that all of Hardy's novels are of a piece, that each is worthy of consideration. While there is agreement that of the novels of the 1870s *Far from the Madding Crowd* and *The Return of the Native* are superior to the others, there is no suggestion whatever that they are in a 'different league' from the others. It now seems extraordinary that Havelock Ellis should have concluded his long essay on 'Thomas Hardy's Novels' (published in the *Westminster Review*, April 1883) with the confident claim that Hardy 'will scarcely write another novel of the peculiar power, and it might be added, the peculiar weakness, of *Far from the Madding Crowd*'. Ellis appears to be making a prediction that will echo Dr Johnson's enduringly startling claim about the characteristically comic nature of Shakespeare's genius:

> It seems more probable that he will pursue the vein of comedy which began in *The Hand of Ethelberta*, and is, perhaps, the most characteristic outcome of his genius.... What fresh variations are possible within these limits it would not be well to

predict, but it is probable that, of stories in this manner, *A Laodicean* and *Two on a Tower* will not be the last.

Wrong on many counts, but chiefly because Hardy followed *Two on a Tower* with, successively, *The Mayor, The Woodlanders, Tess* and *Jude*. By 1889, when Hardy had written *The Mayor* and *The Woodlanders*, the balance had gone against the comic, and how to describe the dominant type of Hardy's fiction became a reviewer's exercise.

J.M. Barrie, writing in *The Contemporary Review* in 1889, had a thesis and a title, 'Thomas Hardy: The Historian of Wessex', which was to be decisive. 'Wessex' became a criterion of value, as we see when *Desperate Remedies* is demoted, not for being set outside of Wessex (for the first edition's 'Froominster' is obviously Dorchester) but for being 'only a study in other people's methods' (Cox, 1970, p. 160). With *Under the Greenwood Tree*, writes Barrie, 'the Wessex series began'. When *Desperate Remedies* was issued in a second edition in 1889, Hardy changed the town's name to 'Troominster' (Purdy, 1954, p. 5; Gatrell, 1988, pp. 124-5) thus removing the association with Dorchester in the River Frome. From 1889 on there is an inexorable identification – advanced by Hardy as much as by the critics – of Wessex and the best of the novels.

Barrie's title includes the odd term 'historian', and this asserts the primary value of Hardy as a realistic novelist. Apart from R.H. Hutton's notorious misapprehension in *The Spectator* that *Far from the Madding Crowd* (which first appeared anonymously) had been written by George Eliot (see Lerner and Holmstrom, 1968, p. 23; Millgate, 1984, p. 100), there was no particular association of Hardy with Eliot's manner of realistic fiction. We have already seen Havelock Ellis' difficulty, as late as 1883, in placing Hardy, and his prediction that Hardy might develop as a writer of the comedy of manners, in the style of Meredith. Barrie denies the importance in Hardy of the comic, but insists rather on the 'humorous', and then restricts the 'humorous' to Wessex:

A further inducement to the author to continue this memor-
able series [i.e., of Wessex novels], is that when treating of
Wessex life he is a humorist, and that his other novels have
scarcely a glimmer of humour from beginning to end.

(Cox, 1970, p. 166)

The claim is so preposterous that it must have ulterior
motives. For Barrie, Hardy's best novels describe Wessex in
a realistic manner; that is to say, the life of Wessex is rich in
humour and pathos.

Hardy is a novelist of such disturbing, if not desolate,
implication that one could almost excuse the processes of
domestication and emasculation to which critics have sub-
jected him. Among those writing during the 1880s there can
be detected an apprehension, a fear of what Hardy will do
next. This is evident in the constant harking back to *Far from
the Madding Crowd*, and in the frequent claim that Hardy's
fiction has been moving in no particular direction, and has
made little progress. In 1890 Edmund Gosse is secure only
in his celebration of *Far from the Madding Crowd*:

Looking back over sixteen years, it is hard to say whether Mr.
Hardy's genius has developed or not since the publication of
what remains his most famous book.

(Cox, 1970, p. 168)

The Mayor of Casterbridge was almost entirely ignored by
Gosse, and had been very poorly received by reviewers, who
almost all stated their preference for *Far from the Madding
Crowd*.

In the late 1880s Hardy may have realized that if he were
to convince the world that his fiction was developing and
going somewhere, it would be necessary for him not only to
arrive but to provide the signposts. Far too little has been
made, in terms either of Hardy's career or of the theoretical
reflection of English fiction, of his three critical and apo-
logetic interventions between 1888 and 1891. Samuel Chew's

prediction has not been fulfilled, and 'The Profitable Reading of Fiction', 'Candour in English Fiction', and 'The Science of Fiction' must be among the least-known of all writings about fiction by major novelists (Chew, 1921, p. 57). As statements they are not satisfactory, but their very lack of clear purpose and contention should serve to prevent hasty judgement, either on the essays themselves, or on Hardy's novels and his fictional intent. It is instructive to see how seldom Hardy's critics defer to the critical writings of their author, in comparison with, say, the critics of James, or Conrad, or Lawrence. Presumably Hardy's essays must be attributed to consciousness rather than to intuition.

Following the publication of *Tess* and *Jude* (whose reception the theoretical essays were intended to prepare) there occurred, simultaneously, public uproar and critical curfew. The outrage is celebrated: the anecdotes about the Bishop, and the American lady journalist, and sundry other disgusted readers are well known, and Hardy has an honourable place as martyr in the struggle for freedom of artistic expression. What is not well known is that in 1894, in the midst of controversy, Lionel Johnson published a monograph on Hardy whose very title, *The Art of Thomas Hardy*, promised – discreetly, or disdainfully – to overlook the scandal. Johnson informs his readers that he has read *Tess* 'some eight or ten times' (within two years of its publication), and there is nothing vulgar in his qualified response:

> I have read Tess, some eight or ten times: at first, with that ravishment and enthusiasm, which great art, art great in spite of imperfection, must always cause. Still the grandeur of the book, its human tragedy, holds and masters me.... But gradually, difficulties, unfelt under the first spell of enchantment, begin to appear: it were unjust to Mr. Hardy to ignore them.
>
> (Johnson, 1894, pp. 227-8; see also Purdy and Millgate, 1978-88, iv, p. 328)

By retrospective domestication of Hardy's previous novels, some of which had caused consternation when first

published, Johnson is able to attribute to Hardy a particular
temper and attitude to art which have here in *Tess*, and by
implication *only* here, been abandoned:

> The sincerity of the book is indubitable: but the passion of
> revolt has led the writer to renounce his impassive temper;
> and to encounter grave difficulties, in that departure from his
> wonted attitude towards art.

> (Johnson, 1894, pp. 228-9)

Tess remains for Johnson one of Hardy's great novels, and we
may feel ourselves to be witnesses of a polite disclaimer.

Annie Macdonell in her monograph, *Thomas Hardy*, also
published in 1894, engages in similar equivocation, and she
appears to anticipate a 'scholarly text' as a solution to the
readers' unhappiness:

> Very likely a definitive edition of the book is wanted.... [*Tess*
> lays itself open to extreme criticisms] as do not a few of the
> great books of the world, till tradition has raised a fence of
> reverence about them, and they become fetishes....

> (Macdonell, 1894, p. 57)

Annie Macdonell deserves commendation for having fore-
seen the Hardy industry as a form of fetish-worship. The
tempers and passions of the public debate about Hardy in the
1890s have indeed been safely excluded from the critical
tradition, filtered out in the move from reviews to monographs, from controversy to canonicity.

Macdonell dissolves ideological embarrassment in two
propositions: that 'the distinctly intellectual quality of his
genius has hardly been adequately recognized' (Macdonell,
1894, p. 9); and that (as we saw in ch. 1) 'he comes nearer to
having the vision and using the methods of a painter than
any other novelist one could name' (Macdonell, 1894, p. 16).
Johnson, likewise, avoids controversy by putting Hardy
within a tradition of novelists who may not be distinctly
intellectual, but who are already and explicitly dead:

Among the dead English novelists of our century, there are...seven names so far above mediocrity, that we can only call them great. These are Scott, Miss Austen, Dickens, Thackeray, Charlotte Brontë, Emily Brontë, and George Eliot.

(Johnson, 1894, p. 25)

Johnson goes on to assert that 'the more ancient novel' ends with Thackeray, and – reviving the *Spectator*'s informed guess – the 'modern novel' begins with George Eliot, whose distinguished successor is Hardy (Johnson, 1894, p. 26). He is concerned with the reputation of the novel, so that his title, *The Art of Thomas Hardy*, although ideologically defusing, is also polemical: had any other novelist, before 1894, had his or her 'art' so prominently flaunted in the title of a critical work? (This is not the same as the 'art of fiction', to allude to James' essay of 1884 – or to Walter Besant's earlier essay, whose title James echoes to rebuke – in which 'art' still denotes 'craft' or 'technique'.) In the 1880s Henry Holbeach, in an essay touching on Hardy, could write (in the summary of Edmund Blunden) that 'between 1860 and 1880 the novel had developed astonishingly, and could now be considered, as a principle means of expression, alongside poetry and philosophy' (Blunden, 1942, p. 44). Johnson has to explain why a writer of such 'art' as Hardy should be a novelist:

His chosen method of expression is the novel: that method, which, since the days of Elizabeth and of the Stuarts, has more and more won for itself a high and serious consideration: so that it is commonly recognized in our times, as the characteristic method of presentation, for the high play of motives and adventures.... I see, in this universal triumph of the novel, no sign of a wholly new order of things for artistic treatment; but a sign, that with an increased conflict and complexity in the old play of human life with life, art has established, by means of the novel, a new and lively convenience for giving to that play a form.

(Johnson, 1894, p. 12)

The eerie ambiguity of 'the old play of human life with life' gives pre-eminence, in Johnson's valuation of the novels, to the group he designates as 'Tragic':

> The *Tragic* group comprises; besides *Desperate Remedies*, an early failure of much promise; the six books upon which Mr. Hardy's readers love to dwell: *The Return of the Native, The Woodlanders, Tess of the d'Urbervilles, The Mayor of Casterbridge, Far from the Madding Crowd*, and *A Pair of Blue Eyes*.
>
> (Johnson, 1894, p. 37)

The second group, comprising *Under the Greenwood Tree* and *The Trumpet-Major*, he calls the 'Idyllic', and to the third group, for which he can find no exact label, Johnson consigns *The Hand of Ethelberta, Two on a Tower*, and *A Laodicean*.

By turning a thematic or generic system of classification into a means of evaluation, Johnson's specification of the 'major' works has survived for a century. The only exception would be *A Pair of Blue Eyes* which, for Johnson, presents 'the play of human life with life' through its architectural composition and 'unity of effect':

> ...you can no more miss a sentence, or give some hurried minutes to a chapter, than you can appreciate the proportions of a great Palladian building, if you omit to notice one of its orders. This unity of effect is...the distinction of Mr. Hardy.
>
> (Johnson, 1894, p. 43)

While acknowledging that a number of novels could be claimed as Hardy's masterpiece, Johnson, with his appreciation of unity and design, has an easy choice:

> I readily confess, that I can as little question the pre-eminence of *The Return of the Native*, among Mr. Hardy's works, as that of *King Lear*, among Shakespeare's plays.
>
> (Johnson, 1894, p. 43)

For Johnson, valuing Hardy for his art and the aesthetics of unity, *The Return of the Native* is the great novel. For those who value Hardy as the historian of Wessex, the laurels go to *Far from the Madding Crowd*. Only the ordinary reader, innocent of such defensive strategies, would admit, or have no choice but to concede, the surpassing qualities of *Tess* and *Jude*.

Johnson and Macdonell had, of course, completed their studies before the publication of *Jude*. And Hardy's last novel, coupled with his realization that *Jude* was to be his last novel, seems to have halted the monographic mode of critical assessment. Hardy had been difficult to categorize as a novelist; with the appearance of the poetry and then, in three volumes over the years 1903-8, *The Dynasts*, one can understand the reluctance of critics to commit themselves to generalizations, let alone to conclusions. Even so, it is remarkable that after the two monographs of 1894 there is not another until 1911.

Hardy disconcerted all his admirers by insisting, from 1896 onwards, that he had a low opinion of his fiction, and that he was now going to devote himself to poetry. He also devoted considerable energy to the revising of his novels and stories for a collected edition (Purdy, 1954, pp. 279-82; Gatrell, 1988, pp. 118-40). Between 1894 and 1896 Hardy was writing new prefaces for each of the novels: collectively all sixteen volumes (including short stories) were to be called 'The Wessex Novels' (not to be confused with the 'Wessex Edition' of 1912-13), and the revisions and brief prefaces play up to Barrie's title, 'Historian of Wessex'. This is most blatant in the preface of 1895 to *Far from the Madding Crowd*, but can be noted also in his mention of 'that traditionary King of Wessex – Lear' (1895, *The Return of the Native*; this detail is anticipated in the 1892 Preface to *Tess*), the phrase 'these novels of Wessex life' (1896, *A Laodicean*), in 'my Exhibition of Wessex life' (1895, *The Mayor*), and his disingenuous conclusion to the long preface to *Wessex Tales* (only that to *Far from the Madding Crowd* is longer): 'However, the stories are but dreams, and not records'.

The 1895-6 edition arranges the volumes in no particular order, and demonstrates absolutely no interest in making any distinctions among the novels, whether thematic, generic or evaluative. If Hardy wanted to serve his novels ill, to the advantage of his as yet unpublished poetry, he had found effective means. Hardy had of course been much praised for his settings, for his delineations of the West Country, but nobody had ever taken such local and regional detail for a limitation. In 1901, however, confronted with the 'Wessex Novels', and their prefaces of predominantly topographical concern, W.H. Mallock has to explain that this 'limitation' is only apparent:

> Mr. Hardy's defects...are due entirely to the limitations of his practical knowledge. His knowledge is sure and accurate as regards one class only. It is apt to fail him when he goes further: but of this class – the peasantry of the South of England – his knowledge is extraordinary; and it is allied with an insight into human nature which has enabled him to give universal significance to characters and incidents which *at first sight seem narrow in their marked provincialism.*

> (Lerner and Holmstrom, 1968, p. 161; italics added)

'At first sight', that is, of 'The Wessex Novels', because no earlier reviewers or essayists had had to make such an apology, nor could they have presumed to such condescension. It was precisely Hardy's intention to confirm the unimportance of his fiction by seizing the aesthetic and cosmopolitan high ground with his poetry and *The Dynasts*. Unfortunately, the continuing popularity of the novels, now marked with provincialism, has held, even to the present, the note of condescension.

In June 1911, with *The Dynasts* completed and three volumes of poetry published, Hardy was again concerned about the novels that he was no longer writing. The 'Wessex Edition' which reissued the novels in 1912 retained the name of Wessex, included a map, and emphasized the documentary aspect by replacing the engravings by Henry Macbeth Raeburn, for the 'Wessex Novels', with a photograph as frontispiece for each volume. The most consequential innovation, however, was that proposed in Hardy's letter to his publisher on 24 June 1911:

> My idea for a long time has been to divide the novels into two groups, putting into the second group 4 or 5 of the more superficial & experimental ones, written just for the moment, critics having a way of pitching upon one or other of these lighter ones as typical of the whole. It will make no difference except in the order of numbering & not much in that.

(Purdy and Millgate, 1978-88, iv, p. 160)

The novels and stories were eventually divided into four categories: 'Novels of Character and Environment', 'Romances and Fantasies', 'Novels of Ingenuity' and 'Mixed Novels' (the latter formed a class whose single member, *A Changed Man*, was actually a volume of short stories). In the first category, whose very title alludes to the critical praise of 'unity of effect' and 'the play of human life with life', are the six novels that have subsequently been recognized almost universally as the major ones: *Tess of the d'Urbervilles, Far from the Madding Crowd, Jude the Obscure, The Return of the Native, The Mayor of Casterbridge* and *The Woodlanders*. Also in this group are two volumes of stories, *Life's Little Ironies* and *Wessex Tales*, and the most popular of all the 'lesser' novels, *Under the Greenwood Tree*. Why this is not in the next category is a mystery: it surely belongs, if we must classify, among the 'Romances and Fantasies' with *A Pair of Blue Eyes, The Trumpet-Major, Two on a Tower, The Well-Beloved* and *A Group of Noble Dames*. 'Novels of Ingenuity' is a convenient term with which to push into the background the three novels which had probably attracted the least notice, and which were most often cited with pejorative intent: *Desperate Remedies, The Hand of Ethelberta* and *A Laodicean* (Millgate, 1978; Gatrell, 1988, pp. 175-84).

Anyone even glancingly acquainted with Hardy criticism at any time in the past 80 years can see the effect of Hardy's divisions. These effects are, I should venture, almost entirely deleterious. Nobody in 1912 thought less of the greatest living writer in the English language (in which terms he was frequently praised) because some of his novels were less good than others. But now that Hardy has sanctioned the effective exclusion of the 'Novels of Ingenuity' nobody feels any obligation to read them, and to show an interest in them is to be, as it were, disloyal to the author. Thus the novels which Havelock Ellis in 1883 thought might be the pattern of Hardy's later and greatest work, have by 1912 been pushed aside, treated as irrelevant to the structure and development of Hardy's fiction (see Abercrombie, 1912, ch. 2).

The dishonesty of Hardy's June 1911 letter to Macmillan is compounded in the 'General Preface to the Novels and Poems' dated October 1911, printed in Volume One (*Tess*) of the Wessex Edition, but now reprinted with each and every one of Hardy's novels available currently in the paperback series of Macmillan and Penguin. There is no evidence to suggest that Hardy had been thinking of classifying his novels under different headings until 1911; there is absolutely no reason to suppose that such distinctions were in his mind at the time of writing and publishing each novel. The General Preface begins thus:

> In accepting a proposal for a definite edition of these productions in prose and verse I have found an opportunity of classifying the novels under heads that show approximately the author's aim, if not his achievement, in each book of the series at the date of its composition. Sometimes the aim was lower than at other times; sometimes, where the intention was primarily high, force of circumstances (among which the chief were the necessities of magazine publication) compelled a modification, great or slight, of the original plan. Of a few, however, of the longer novels, and of many of the shorter tales, it may be assumed that they stand to-day much as they would have stood if no accidents had obstructed the channel between the writer and the public. That many of them, if any, stand as they would stand if written *now* is not to be supposed.

In the classification of these fictitious chronicles – for which the name of 'The Wessex Novels' was adopted, and is still retained – the first group is called 'Novels of Character and Environment,' and contains those which approach most nearly to uninfluenced works....

(Orel, 1966. p. 44)

This preface would not stand up to cross-examination. Who is to get the credit or the blame? Is it the paucity of Hardy's ambition, or magazine serialization, or other obstructions? After the fact of writing, is it just a coincidence that the novels which suffered the most in the composition or in the publication are all 'Novels of Ingenuity'? Did it just so happen that the 'unobstructed' and 'uninfluenced' works were all concerned with 'Character and Environment'? Hardy might like us to believe that without obstructions and modifications all fourteen novels would have been worthy of the first class, but then he should not be referring us to aims and intentions, nor should he expect us to believe that the 'Novels of Ingenuity' were 'written for the nonce simply'.

Such a farrago imposes no obligation, no sense of responsibility on the reader's part beyond that of concentrating on the 'Novels of Character and Environment'. Indeed, Hardy tells us that the only reason for re-issuing the novels 'written for the nonce simply' is because 'some of their scenes are not without fidelity to life' (Orel, 1966, p. 45). They therefore partake in the 'verisimilitude' and accuracy that is commended in the 'better' novels. He devotes over one page, out of six, to topographical data, and compares himself with Boswell in his devotion to the fact:

Yet I have instituted inquiries to correct tricks of memory, and striven against temptations to exaggerate, in order to preserve for my own satisfaction a fairly true record of a vanishing life.

(Orel, 1966, p. 46)

That last phrase, cited or paraphrased hundred of times, not only sealed the canonical approach to Hardy as the 'Historian of Wessex' but initiated a critical stream that would make Hardy's chief concern the vanishing of the rural way of life – and the reading of Hardy's fiction too often an escapism. This would find encouragement in the sepia-toned photographs that, as frontispiece, most blatantly obstruct the channel between writer and reader. Furthermore, Hermann Lea's *Thomas Hardy's Wessex*, with 240 photographs of the 'original' places from which 'Wessex' was constructed, goes through the novels, one by one, in the order and classification in which they are issued in the Wessex Edition. Lea's book, first published in 1913, was bound and issued in matching format with the edition to which it was presumably an important key.

There was, then, not so much a hiatus in the monographic criticism between 1894 and 1912 as a respectful silence while Hardy's own utterances and stratagems were being observed. Lascelles Abercrombie, in what remains one of the most urbane and stylish works on Hardy, is in no doubt about the hierarchical arrangement of the novels. He discusses *Desperate Remedies*, *A Pair of Blue Eyes*, *The Hand of Ethelberta*, *A Laodicean* and *The Well-Beloved* in a chapter starkly titled 'Minor Novels'. Those which we enjoy reading, even though they fail to be 'major', *Under the Greenwood Tree*, *The Trumpet-Major* and *Two on a Tower*, are gathered with the short stories as 'Annexes'. Under 'Dramatic Form' Abercrombie includes four of 'the six great novels which form the main building, in our architectural image' (Abercrombie, 1912, ch. 5); *Far from the Madding Crowd*, *The Return of the Native*, *The Mayor of Casterbridge* and *The Woodlanders* are dramatic because they involve centrally more than one character:

> ...the action is a woven intricacy of many curving and recurving lines, carrying the threaded lives of several persons through a single complicated pattern of destiny....

> (Abercrombie, 1912, p. 103)

By contrast *Tess* and *Jude* (and the contrast is more convincing in the former than the latter) are concerned with a single person and are therefore best described as having 'epic form':

> The difference between the two sets of novels is the difference between a history of an individual, and a history of the relationship in a group of individuals; and from this thematic difference, formal difference naturally follows.

(Abercrombie, 1912, p. 104)

Abercrombie has a good sense of the relatedness of form and theme; he even hints that architecture is present in all the novels, as structure in the good ones, as theme (using 'personal experience to supply the failure of inspiration') in the minor ones.

Although Jude Fawley is not to the same degree as Tess the sole focus of narrative attention, Abercrombie's point expresses the sense that their two novels are distinct, and need separate consideration, without fault necessarily being found in them. Instead of condemning *Tess* and *Jude* for their polemical purpose, or for sacrificing form to propaganda, Abercrombie allows that authorial intervention is not 'commentary' on the story and therefore extrinsic to it, but may have its own artistic value. In Hardy's novels of 'dramatic form' the narrator represents but does not utter his opinion on the desirability or otherwise of what is represented:

> But there are artists who are unable to remain content with an art which holds this strictly judicial attitude to their own conclusions; their summing up of life's conduct strongly moves them...and this also at last demands artistic expression.
>
> Herein, it appears, lies the secret of Hardy's change from fiction of dramatic to fiction of epic form. The aesthetic manner of those four great novels...enabled him to express his intellectual conception of life.... But it withheld him from adding to his formation of life the gloss of his own opinion of the tragedy.... Already, in *The Mayor of Casterbridge*, Hardy

appears somewhat restive under the restriction; the book seems several times on the verge of indignantly protesting against the injustice of Henchard's fate.... One has the feeling that the art is here constantly hoping to be able to do something which the artist's conscience will not tolerate. So a change of aesthetic habit becomes necessary, and *Tess of the d'Urbervilles* and *Jude the Obscure* are written in a form which the artist's conscience easily allows to contain an emotional as well as an intellectual judgment of life.

(Abercrombie, 1912, pp. 130-1)

In an unguarded moment Abercrombie reveals the lack of conviction in his own argument. *Tess* is weakened by the absence of any richly drawn character apart from the heroine herself: Abercrombie devotes some lively pages to the denunciation of Angel Clare, 'the only one of Hardy's characters who is genuinely odious', but, in spite of his best hatred, Abercrombie finds it hard not to see Angel and Alex as attenuatingly allegorical. The power of *Jude*, however, lies in the presentation of Arabella and Sue, and the novel in this aspect belongs with those labelled 'Dramatic':

In these two women, and their relationship with the finer faculties of Jude's mind, the real tragedy is placed; and they are drawn with as minute and scrupulous accuracy, and hold as important a position in the main theme, as Jude himself. The book therefore has a decidedly richer humanity than *Tess of the d'Urbervilles*.

(Abercrombie, 1912, p. 159)

Abercrombie concludes his treatment of Hardy's novels with a subtle discussion of Hardy's metaphysic and its formal properties; this is necessary if aesthetic evaluation is to be more than a matter of opinion:

...to fix its value to the 'truth' of its conceptions, the pleasantness of its tone, or the usefulness, moral or otherwise, of its purport, is only to make it endlessly debatable. But the interests of moral usefulness and complete formality will not often be in opposition – they certainly are not in Hardy; for genuine morality is but a kind of shapeliness.

(Abercrombie, 1912, pp. 167-8)

Here is a sophisticated aesthetic at the service of a broad tolerance: Beach aside, very few Hardy critics, even in books far longer than Abercrombie's, have given any space to *The Romantic Adventures of a Milkmaid*, which he finds to be more 'genuinely characteristic' of Hardy than *A Laodicean*: 'The romantic apparatus is, to be sure, somewhat preposterous; but it is quite pleasantly preposterous...' (Abercrombie, 1912, p.69).

Abercrombie's is of course the first monograph in which the fiction has to share space with the poetry and *The Dynasts*. Abercrombie is most disappointing on the poetry, as if unable to consider it anything but a novelist's distraction; to *The Dynasts*, however, he allots forty pages, almost one quarter of his book. For whatever reason, perhaps chiefly because of the still dubious status of the novel, and also because of the economics of patriotism, *The Dynasts* was more highly regarded during Hardy's lifetime than it has been since, and the early commentators are often more perceptive in their sympathy than the later ones in their condescension.

Abercrombie notices that the Pities are so horrified by what they see that they are forced to assume that there must be some good at the end of it all:

> The Ironies, on the other hand, take existence as an enjoyable comedy; but they can only do so by enjoying the perfection of the malice which they suppose is at the bottom of the world's affairs.

(Abercrombie, 1912, p. 201)

His discussion of the Spirits Ironic seems to anticipate Walter Benjamin's understanding of fascism as the aestheticization of politics. Abercrombie is not interested in *The Dynasts* for its treatment of history and of the Napoleonic era; he is drawn rather to its analysis of moral and psychological perversions of consciousness:

> ...the delighted pessimism of the Ironies may seem fantastic. It is not that really, however; nothing is more certain psychologically, than man's perversely pleasurable excitement by what goes counter to his notions of rightness. To enjoy the worldly spectacle because it seems managed by a purpose of deliberate cruelty, is the sublimation of this perversity. The queer complexity of modern consciousness could not be better exhibited than in these spirits of tragic optimism and amused pessimism.

> (Abercrombie, 1912, p. 202)

As with *Tess* and *Jude*, Abercrombie resists discussion of the ideas detached from aesthetic form:

> As a philosophy of existence, it would be very easy to say that this will not do. As a tragedy of existence, it is surely magnificent, a profoundly enjoyable shapeliness of idea, nobly familiar to the desires of consciousness.

> (Abercrombie, 1912, p. 210)

That last phrase, connecting 'noble' with 'desire' in the context of the 'perversions' of consciousness, not only has implications, but may explain why readers, even Hardy's admirers, are so reluctant to address *The Dynasts*.

If Hardy's General Preface to the Wessex Edition has served his fiction poorly, that is because his aim was to enhance the relative worth of his poetry and *The Dynasts*. Hardy made an attempt to justify the limited scope of his topography by arguing that 'there was quite enough human nature in Wessex for one man's literary purpose', and that it would have been easy for him to have given 'more cosmopolitan features to the narrative.' (See Orel, 1966, p. 45.) This sounds defensive, as if Hardy were having to answer charges of provincialism. We have already seen that merely by giving so much attention to the topographical aspect, Hardy was inviting critics to read his novels in the light of such charming picture-books as Wilkinson Sherren's *The Wessex of Romance* (1902), and of Hermann Lea's book, effectively an appendage to the Wessex Edition. By 1911 Hardy could afford to boast that he need not have confined himself to one region, that he could have been more cosmopolitan, because the evidence for that is now available in *The Dynasts*. Yet Hardy makes no such claim for *The Dynasts*, suggesting rather, in the same preface, that the optical experimentation in that work may permit readers to charge it also with provincialism:

> To be sure, one might argue that by surveying Europe from a celestial point of vision...that continent becomes virtually a province – a Wessex, an Attica, even a mere garden – and hence is made to conform to the principle of the novels, however far it outmeasures their region. But that may be as it will.

> (Orel, 1966, p. 48)

Behind the concern for topographical equivalence and for the true record of a vanishing life this point gets lost, or sentimentalized. Sentimentality occurs when critics *justify* provincialism by reference to the depth and scope of one human heart, and to the corresponding unimportance of high politics and international affairs.

Hardy's point, however, is concerned with optics and the point of viewing or of vision. This was apprehended by Harold Child in a modest-seeming study, *Thomas Hardy*, in the series 'Writers of the Day', published in 1916. Child's theme is what in Hardy 'might be called his double vision':

> If he sees the littleness, he sees also the greatness. Watching from infinity, he shows human life as futile and trivial...[yet] There is no trace in his work of contempt for human will, endurance and passion.... In this double vision of man's

greatness and man's futility lies the secret of Hardy's tragedy.

(Child, 1916, pp. 21-2)

Sentimentality is avoided only because vision is not allowed metaphorical lease, but remains bound to optics. This is most impressively so, unsurprisingly, in *The Dynasts*, for which book Hardy will, according to Child, be best known to future generations (Child, 1916, p. 83). Child makes a telling objection to Granville Barker's staging of scenes from *The Dynasts* in November 1914, when the work was summoned to help the war effort:

> ...its poetic unity, in fact all the *bigness* of it – these were lost. The proportions were destroyed. Man became huge and the heavens were tucked away in corners.

(Child, 1916, p. 92)

Child takes 'double vision' to be Hardy's characteristic, and then argues that *The Dynasts* is superior to the fiction insofar as Hardy has gone beyond doubleness to multiplicity of vision:

> The vision in *The Dynasts* has become multiple.... The Phantom Intelligences...have a technical as well as philosophical use, for they preserve, better, perhaps, than the celestial beings in any other epic, the idea of the infinite possibility of visual adjustment.

(Child, 1916, p. 106)

'The infinite possibility of visual adjustment' looks forward in general to the sense of complexity and disunity in Hardy's art of the most recent critics; and more narrowly Child anticipates the observation that Hardy was, as it were, working conceptually with the as yet undeveloped optical possibilities of cinema.

In terms of evaluating the fiction, Child agrees with the primacy accorded by Abercrombie to the novels of 'dramatic form': these are the four novels 'still most commonly accepted as the crown of Hardy's work. *Tess* and *Jude* have still their irreconcilable enemies; the poems and *The Dynasts* have not yet come into their own.' (See Child, 1916, p. 56.) Indeed the reputation of *Tess* and *Jude* remained controversial. Herbert Grimsditch was the first to notice, in 1925, that *Jude the Obscure* 'has been described by different critics as the worst and the greatest of Hardy's novels' (Grimsditch, 1925, p. 155). The critic to whom Grimsditch alludes for high praise of *Jude* is H.C. Duffin, whose *Thomas Hardy: A Study of the Wessex Novels, the Poems and The Dynasts*, much reprinted and revised, was first published in 1916. Duffin later changed his opinion, and decided that *Tess* was Hardy's greatest novel, having a 'tense rhythm' and a constant emotional centre. *Jude* has too many irreconcilables that might be irrelevances: 'it admits purely episodic events, such as the comedy scene of Jude and the hymn-writer' (Duffin, 1964, p. 77). The advantage of that uncertainty as to what the novel's centre *is* lies in our held attention:

> There is no end to the meaning and inspiration of *Jude the Obscure*.... The problem of *Tess* is more soluble: we may decide and leave it, grieving or rejoicing. But there is no solving *Jude*. It wakes dim enigmas; it starts strange trains of unanswerable question....
>
> (Duffin, 1964, p. 77)

In no one more, perhaps, were dim enigmas stirred than in D.H. Lawrence, whose *Study of Thomas Hardy* was written in the latter half of 1914, although not published until 1936. It is normal to say of this extraordinary essay that it tells us much about Lawrence and very little about Hardy. That is an understandable response to an essay whose title is so blatantly misleading. Had the Nietzschean title by which Lawrence referred to this essay, 'Le Gai Savaire', been retained, it is likely that its 'few brilliant pages on Hardy' would have been more celebrated, and more valued in the critical tradition.

The essay's re-issue in 1985 (the Cambridge Edition of the Works of D.H. Lawrence) provides a critical apparatus that enables us to see more clearly Lawrence's place in the development of writings about Hardy. According to the editor, Bruce Steele, Lawrence was responding not directly to Hardy's novels, but to Abercrombie's monograph (Lawrence, 1985, pp. xxvii-xxix). On first reading Abercrombie, Lawrence had been impressed by his conjunction of aesthetics and metaphysics:

> The highest art must have a metaphysic.... And Thomas Hardy, by deliberately putting the art of his fiction under the control of a metaphysic, has thereby made the novel capable of the highest service to man's consciousness.
>
> (Abercrombie, 1912, pp. 19-20)

Hardy's use of metaphysics is, for Abercrombie in 1912, the clue to the greatness of his novels, just as the extravagance of the metaphysical structure accounts for the surpassing achievement of *The Dynasts*. Initially favourable, Lawrence came to disagree with Abercrombie about the value of metaphysics in Hardy's work. Lawrence acknowledged its presence but found it vitiating. From the second edition of his book in 1919 Abercrombie omitted six pages, including the substance of his discussion of Hardy's metaphysics. Lawrence's views, though unpublished, must have been conveyed to Abercrombie, who was presumably persuaded. What for Lawrence lends Hardy distinction is 'his feeling, his instinct, his sensuous understanding' (Lawrence, 1985, p. 93), all of which had, for Abercrombie in 1912, been restrained by the metaphysic and thus given aesthetic form. For Lawrence, Hardy is at his best when he escapes from his own ideas: 'and turning to the earth, to the landscape, then he is true to himself.' (Lawrence, 1985, p. 93.) Abercrombie's concern with Hardy's metaphysic puts Lawrence in mind of Tolstoy's metaphysical theories of history and ethics: 'The theory of knowledge, the metaphysic of the man, is much smaller than the man himself. So with Tolstoi.'

The comparison is important. Readers of *War and Peace* have often been encouraged to skip the chapters of historiographical theorizing, and critics have often written studies of the novel without mentioning those (numerous) chapters. Readers and critics thus undertake a salvage operation, and the effort is justified because of the vitality, sensual apprehension, feeling of lived experience in the 'main' part of *War and Peace*. As *The Dynasts* shared with *War and Peace* the subject of the Napoleonic Wars the connection between Hardy and Tolstoy was inescapable from 1903 onwards. Subsequently the comparison would be drawn between Tolstoy and Hardy as novelists, both to proclaim Hardy's stature and to excuse his flaws. Lawrence cites Tolstoy saying of *Anna Karenina*, and in defence of that novel's moral and metaphysical burden: 'what difficulty is there in writing about how an officer fell in love with a married woman?... there's no difficulty in it, and, above all, no good in it' (Lawrence, 1985, p. 92). To this Lawrence adds: 'And Thomas Hardy's metaphysic is something like Tolstoi's.' Now of course Lawrence would find no greater challenge than to describe an officer falling in love with a married woman; its difficulty and its goodness would be equally self-evident. At the time of writing the *Study of Thomas Hardy* Lawrence was engaged on his most ambitious work, *The Sisters*, that we know as two novels: *The Rainbow* and *Women in Love*. And while these novels of Lawrence also carry a considerable 'burden' of moral and philosophical weight – even a metaphysic – they are not susceptible to the process of partition and division in the reading process which would separate the description from the philosophy, or the vitality from the vitalism.

Lawrence, after all, has just as much to say as do Hardy and Tolstoy – he is as 'opinionated' as they, if not more so – and he learnt, from the failure of Hardy's metaphysic, how to integrate his novels. In other words, Lawrence's attack on Hardy's metaphysic, and on Abercrombie's claim for its importance, is motivated by Lawrence's need to find Hardy inadequate, that there might be room for Lawrence to do better. As has been said of Lawrence's first novel, *The White Peacock* (1911), its basic purpose is 'to be a Hardy novel that shows Hardy was wrong' (Murfin, 1978, p. 188). But having looked at Hardy's novels and at their early reception, we can see that Lawrence's complaint is virtually unprecedented. It was Abercrombie who, writing after the publication of *The Dynasts*, was the first to attribute a metaphysic to Hardy, and that attribution was, for Lawrence, a convenient label for whatever was wrong with Hardy. Could Lawrence have written *The Rainbow* and *Women in Love* without having thus 'identified' Hardy's weakness? It would be wrong, however, to regard the *Study of Thomas Hardy* as of merely symptomatic interest, a document in and of the creative development of D. H. Lawrence. With his determination to ignore Hardy's metaphysic (which is anyway hard to find) goes a contempt for what other critics have applauded in Hardy, the artistic form of the novels; and that contempt is made convincing by Lawrence's conflation of form and plot. No critic has ever located Hardy's greatness centrally in his plots.

Hardy's greatness, for Lawrence, is to be found in his characters, and in his characters' connection with the earth. That connection or rootedness enables them to live not by reason or law but by feeling, passion and sensuality. In opposing Abercrombie's stress on metaphysic, which finally subordinates the novels to *The Dynasts*, Lawrence is doing nothing radical, for he is restoring the emphases of Hardy's own classification: character and environment. On Clym Yeobright, Lawrence is memorably unforgiving (and he cannot have known of Hardy's sympathetic predilection for this character as reported by F. E. Hardy in 1928):

> What is Clym's altruism but a deep very subtle cowardice, that makes him shirk his own being whilst apparently acting nobly; which makes him choose to improve mankind rather than to struggle at the quick of himself into being. He is not able to undertake his own soul, so he will take a commission for society to enlighten the souls of others.... He had never become an integral man, because when faced with the de-

mand to produce himself, he remained under cover of the community and excused by his altruism.

(Lawrence, 1985, p. 24)

'Altruism' for Lawrence is a morality that is an alibi for not living in and for oneself. Altruism requires people to communicate cerebrally, and by words, not through matter and bodies: Clym 'is left preaching, out of sheer emptiness' (Lawrence, 1985, p. 24). Opposed to altruism is the sense of community in which people are related through their sharing of earth, by autochthony:

> The earth heaved with raw instinct, Egdon whose dark soil was strong and crude and organic as the body of a beast. Out of the body of this crude earth are born Eustacia, Wildeve, Mistress Yeobright, Clym, and all the others.

(Lawrence, 1985, p. 25)

There is, then, in Lawrence a metaphysic, and an ethic. The ethic is to be like the earth that produced you, or (wherein Clym fails) to produce yourself as you have already been produced by Egdon. Eustacia is Lawrence's ideal, in spite of the fact that in her desire for Paris she does not understand that the Heath 'is under Paris as well as under Wessex', and that therefore she has no need to go there: her real Paris, the place of her desire, is 'beside some strong-passioned, unconfined man, her mate' (Lawrence, 1985, p. 26). Clym's mistake is to live according to system and convention, and to expect Eustacia to fit into his system:

> He did not know that Eustacia had her being beyond him. He did not know that she existed untouched by his system and his mind, where no system had sway and where no consciousness had risen to the surface. He did not know that she was Egdon, the powerful, eternal origin seething with production.

(Lawrence, 1985 p. 27)

It does not escape Lawrence that there are others who are
content with Egdon, who have constructed no system for
themselves, and who are barely conscious, yet who fall far
short of the Lawrentian ideal:

> Thomasin and Venn have nothing in them turbulent enough
> to push them to the bounds of the convention. There is always
> room for them inside. They are genuine people, and they get
> the prize within the walls.

> (Lawrence, 1985, p. 24)

Lawrence makes much of these 'walls' but never quite reconciles the two commandments: that one be identified with the
Heath and be unconsciously, passionately productive with
the Heath, and also that one recognize the walls of convention, law and order, and break out of them.

If this is unreasonable it is at least consonant with the
Heath, and with those admirable characters who are as
irrational as their origin. And we can play a familiar trick on
Lawrence by ignoring his pretentious theories and specious
arguments, the better to appreciate his insights into Hardy's
characters. Critics who value the nuances of consciousness
and conscience that motivate and explain behaviour in the
novels of James or Meredith, Woolf or Conrad, are often the
first to express impatience with Hardy. Lawrence presents
Hardy's characters as rather more irrational and inconse-
quential in their behaviour than other readers have supposed; and he does this by taking an extreme position against
those who like their fictional characters to possess psychological consistency and plausibility.

> It is urged against Thomas Hardy's characters that they do
> unreasonable things – quite, quite unreasonable things. They
> are always going off unexpectedly and doing something that
> nobody would do. That is quite true, and the charge is amus-
> ing. These people of Wessex are always bursting suddenly out
> of bud and taking a wild flight into flower, always shooting
> something out of a tight convention, a tight, hide-bound

cabbage state into something quite madly personal.... Nowhere, except perhaps in Jude, is there the slightest development of personal action in the characters.

(Lawrence, 1985, p. 20)

It seems hardly worth sorting out all the contradictions in
this passage, but it is worth noting the contrast between
Jude's 'development of personal action' and the state of those
who have burst out, which is 'quite madly personal'. The
latter may be, rather, the negation of the personal; in the leap
from cabbage to flower one switches stereotypes, and demonstrates the unreliability of stereotypes, but one does not
necessarily achieve personality. If we take the titles of the
books in *Tess* we find precisely this pattern: 'The Maiden',
'Maiden No More', 'The Woman Pays'. We do not have, even
with Tess, and much less with Bathsheba or Grace, Clym or
Henchard, that 'consecutive' development of personality to
which Dorothea Brook and Isabel Archer may have accus-
tomed us.

Lawrence is using Hardy to advance his own theory of the
breakdown of 'the old stable ego', and it is a moot point
whether Hardy actually justifies the case, or whether subsequent critics have not been reading Lawrence rather than
Hardy. The contemporary French philosopher, critic and
psychologist, Gilles Deleuze, who has explored the fragmen-
tation of personality in such radical works (written with Felix
Guattari) as *Anti-Oedipus* and *A Thousand Plateaus*, has
this to say of Hardy:

> ...his characters are not people or subjects, they are collec-
> tions of intensive sensations, each is such a collection, a
> packet, a bloc of variable sensations. There is a strange
> respect for the individual, an extraordinary respect: not be-
> cause he would seize upon himself as a person and be recog-
> nized as a person, in the French way, but on the contrary
> because he saw himself and saw others as so many 'unique
> chances' – the unique chance from which one combination or
> another had been drawn. Individuation without a subject.

And these packets of sensations in the raw, these collections
or combinations, run along the lines of chance, or mis-
chance.... Individuals, packets of sensation, run over the
heath like a line of flight or a line of deterritorialization of the
earth.

(Deleuze and Parnet, 1987, pp. 39-40)

Deleuze has taken the Lawrentian idea of the unreality or
'fiction' of the old unitary self, and has postulated the individual in terms of *bricolage*, random or contingent assemb-
lages of instincts, sensations and passions. The 'unique
chance' – and nothing else – constitutes individuation, and
Deleuze takes Hardy's characters to exemplify this reduction
of personality (Deleuze and Parnet, 1987, pp. 51 ff.).

Whether one agrees with Deleuze is not the issue here.
Lawrence's words on Hardy have a certain visionary force
that quite transcends the context of his less than logical
argument. He is one of the few writers to have responded to
Hardy in words of intensity and extravagance and conviction.
It is whimsical that Deleuze should take Hardy as typical of
the English novel, in contrast to the French novel with its
rational, unified heroes, when Lawrence's view of Hardy is
so atypical, and scarcely figures in the secondary literature.
No doubt as feminist criticism of Hardy avails itself of more
sophisticated theoretical models of gender and subjectivity
(recently Garson and Goode have invoked Lacan) we will
witness a more considered estimate of Lawrence's contribution.

By disdaining not only metaphysics but form as well,
Lawrence powerfully inaugurates the attack on *The Dynasts*
which many reviewers and critics, taking Hardy's cue, acclaimed as his greatest work from the time of its publication
until at least 1928, the year of his death. In February 1928
Edmund Gosse delivered a broadcast eulogy on Hardy in
which he described his works as forming a trilithon, fiction
and poetry being the two supporting pillars with *The Dynasts*
as the crowning architrave. *The Dynasts* fell from this height
shortly afterwards, and the publication of Lawrence's essay

in 1936 only endorsed what was already occurring. Had his animadversions against *The Dynasts* been published 20 years earlier they might have provoked some of that work's champions into a reasoned defence of their enthusiasm. For Lawrence *The Dynasts* is valueless, apparently, because it is all metaphysic and form, and is quite without 'characters':

> If it were not that the man is much stronger in feeling than in thought, the Wessex novels would be sheer rubbish, as they are already in parts. *The Well-Beloved* is sheer rubbish, fatuity, as is a good deal of the *Dynasts* conception.
>
> But it is not as a metaphysician that one must consider Hardy. He makes a poor show there. For nothing in his work is so pitiable as his clumsy efforts to push events into line with his theory of being, and to make calamity fall on those who represent the principle of Love. He does it exceedingly badly, and owing to this effort his form is execrable in the extreme.

> (Lawrence, 1985, p. 93)

Classical, or merely traditional admirers of Hardy found it reassuring to praise *The Dynasts*: an 'epic-drama' combines the most ancient and honoured of literary genres, and is the antithesis of the novel's still unproven novelty. Once 'the novel' was secure as a genre, it was no longer necessary to justify Hardy's novels in terms of *The Dynasts*, nor to celebrate *The Dynasts* as the fulfilment and culmination of the novels.

Lawrence writes with immense confidence in the authority of the novel; indeed, he claims elsewhere that all the greatest works of world literature are novels, and gives as examples the Bible, Homer and Shakespeare (Lawrence, 1985, p. 196). What Lawrence means by 'novel' is a capacious openness so expansive and protean as to resist the taking or holding of any form that could be aesthetically apprehended and appreciated in the classical manner. In thus arguing on Hardy's behalf, Lawrence takes many risks, and renders Hardy extremely vulnerable to his antagonists. For Lawrence disallows any worth in Hardy that partakes of form or philosophy, the two aspects of Hardy's works that had attracted most of the favourable critical attention. Hardy's value is entirely outside aesthetic and intellectual grasp, to be gauged by divination, or however it may be that we dissolve and resolve all components of the text into two elements to which the text is contingent: the earthy and the vatic. Lawrence's attempt to claim Hardy as a prophet has been decidedly unsuccessful; yet as contemporary literary theory learns to address prophetic and visionary texts as *texts* (n.b. the importance of Plotinus, Eckhart, Rousseau, Sade, Pascal, Nietzsche etc., in deconstructive practice) it may be that what Lawrence saw in Hardy has yet to be exposed. Deleuze's enthusiasm for Hardy, informed by Lawrence, should not be regarded as an isolated phenomenon but as part of that profound rethinking of text and discourse in which, oddly, Hardy's voice has been almost entirely mute. Or latent.

3

Literary Transferences: Writers on Hardy from Lawrence to Auden

If we take from Lawrence's *Study of Thomas Hardy* such occasional insights and pithy formulations as suit our critical needs, we domesticate the text. What Lawrence says about the individual novels may have an appropriate context. When that context is manifest, what seems now, in Lawrence's comments on Hardy, irritatingly casual, erratic and wilful – or equally irritating in its bullying insistence – may cohere. Until then we should be provoked by Lawrence's version of *Far from the Madding Crowd,* in which shepherd is likened to sheep-dog, and the power of seduction is a form of knowledge.

> The unruly Bathsheba, though almost pledged to Farmer Boldwood, a ravingly passionate, middle-aged bachelor pretendant, who has suddenly started in mad pursuit of some unreal conception of woman, personified in Bathsheba, lightly runs off and marries Sergeant Troy, an illegitimate aristocrat, unscrupulous and yet sensitive in taking his pleasures. She loves Troy, he does not love her. All the time she is loved faithfully and persistently by the good Gabriel, who is like a dog that watches the bone and bides the time. Troy treats Bathsheba badly, never loves her, though he is the only

man in the book who knows anything about her...enter the
good steady Gabriel, who marries Bathsheba because he will
make her a good husband, and the flower of imaginative fine
love is dead for her with Troy's scorn of her.

(Lawrence, 1985, pp. 22-3)

Lawrence has an extraordinary obsession with class in
Hardy's fiction, and whoever can be deemed 'aristocratic'
wins Lawrence's approval. Gabriel, not being aristocratic,
cannot be the object or subject of 'imaginative fine love';
indeed, 'he will make her a good husband' directs us from a
question of syntax to that of the wearing of trousers: Bathsheba, as she is already her own bailiff, may well become her
own husband.

Lawrence's explanation for Hardy's 'pessimism' is wilful
and ingenious, and almost persuasive. It takes the phenomenon of the 'aristocrat', present in so many novels, and usually
regarded as an intrusive presence – Hardy does best when
he sticks to the workfolk of Wessex that he knows best – and
offers an explanation:

There is all the way through a 'prédilection d'artiste' for the
aristocrat, and all the way through a moral condemnation of
him, a substituting the middle or lower class personage with
bourgeois virtues into his place. This was the root of Hardy's
pessimism. Not until he comes to Tess and Jude does he
sympathize with the aristocrat – unless it be in *The Mayor of
Casterbridge*, and then he sympathizes only to slay.

(Lawrence, 1985, p. 45; the text here is problematic
but it is now clear that Lawrence is not talking
only about *A Laodicean*, as earlier
editions suppose)

Lawrence would be on the side not only of Troy – 'unscrupu-
lous, but discriminative' – but of Alec d'Urberville:

It is, in actual life, a rare man who seeks and seeks among

women for one of such character and intrinsic female being as Tess.... An ordinary sensualist would have been much too common, and much too afraid to turn to Tess. In a way, d'Urberville was her mate.

(Lawrence, 1985, p. 101)

Lawrence thus overturns whatever undermining of Alec's character is implied in his purchase of a title: Alec, in spite of his vulgar new wealth and pretensions, really is an aristocrat. So, even more astonishingly, is Arabella, and if readers have a somewhat mixed impression of these two characters it is due to 'Hardy's bad art'. Lawrence's defence of Arabella follows the pattern of his defence of Alec; only a special person, sensitive, discriminating, aristocratic, would be attracted to Tess or to Jude:

And no ordinary woman would want Jude.... A coarse, shallow woman does not want to marry a sensitive, deep-feeling man.... She wants a man to correspond to herself.... Arabella was, under all her disguise of pig-fat and false hair, and vulgar speech, in character somewhere an aristocrat. She was, like Eustacia, amazingly lawless, even splendidly so.

Hardy's 'bad art' is not just a failure to see the true qualities behind the 'disguise' but it is rather the manipulation of those disguises so that the reader should take them for the reality. In this, Hardy shows his fear of the aristocrat, even while admiration depicts such characters as will, for a reader such as Lawrence, shine through the disguises:

[Hardy] himself, as an artist, manages in the whole picture of Arabella almost to make insignificant in her these pig-sticking false hair crudities. But he must have his personal revenge on her, for her coarseness, which offends him, because he is something of an Angel Clare.

(Lawrence, 1985, p. 101)

Hardy is thus ethically embarrassed by the coarseness which he aesthetically celebrates. This adds complexity to Child's view of Hardy's 'double vision', where the perspective of human grandeur commands an ethical response, and the perspective of human littleness accepts the futility of ethics.

More than that, Lawrence has, implicitly, theorized the contiguity of desire. The reader of *Tess* and *Jude* might suppose that the narrative function of Alec and Arabella was, precisely and merely, to oppose and destroy all that Tess and Jude represent. Because Lawrence speaks, so naively, of fictional characters as real people, he sees Alec and Arabella not as emblems, and not from the protagonist's viewpoint, but as free agents who could be elsewhere. It might be rather more naive, in fact, not to ask, with Lawrence, why Alec and Arabella have become involved with Tess and Jude. In rejecting the 'merely destructive', or the 'merely sensuous', Lawrence asks us to examine what Angelic prudishness lurks in those glib 'merelys'.

In thus conferring some dignity of motive on Alec and Arabella, Lawrence recovers them from emblematic status, and solicits the reader's engaged interest. As Troy had known Bathsheba better than any other man in that novel, so Alec 'came close to [Tess], as Clare could never have done' (Lawrence, 1985, p. 99), and Sue can never know Jude in the body as Arabella had known him. Both Tess and Jude are challenged by Lawrence, as if their failures were their own doing: 'Jude's real desire was, not to live in the body. He wanted to exist only in his mentality. He was as if bored, or blasé, in the body, just like Tess.' In refuting Hardy's metaphysics (the President of the Immortals, etc.), Lawrence insists on reading the novel in the light of Hardy's own beliefs, as Hardy often expressed them publicly. Lawrence holds Hardy accountable for the discrepancy between his proclaimed agnosticism and his exploited metaphysics of tragedy and doom. Given that neither Tess not Hardy can blame 'the President of the Immortals', Lawrence looks for the proper culprit. He contrasts modern with Classical and Shakespearean tragedy, arguing that, in the latter, circumstances are 'unalterable and invincible':

On the other hand, Anna [Karenina], Eustacia, Tess or Sue –
what was there in their position that was necessarily tragic?
Necessarily painful it was, but they were not at war with God,
only with Society. Yet they were all cowed by the mere judgement of man upon them, and all the while by their own souls
they were right. And the judgement of man killed them, not
the judgement of their own souls, or the judgement of eternal
God.

Which is the weakness of modern tragedy, where trans-
gression against the social code is made to bring destruction,
as though the social code worked our irrevocable fate.

(Lawrence, 1985, p. 30)

Critics have always found it more comfortable to treat
Hardy's characters as victims of a metaphysical system, and
then to take issue with the metaphysics. Lawrence's anta-
gonism to Hardy's metaphysics is, we realize, motivated by
a desire to treat Hardy's characters as responsible adults,
and to find them, often, wanting.

Most provocative of all Lawrence's judgements on Hardy's
characters is the extensive treatment of Sue Bridehead.
Against the prevailing assumption that associated *Jude the
Obscure* with novels such as Grant Allen's *The Woman Who
Did* published at the same time, and with the 'topical' question of 'the New Woman', Lawrence sees Sue as far from being
a new or emancipated woman, in fact hardly a woman at all.
She denies both her body and her femaleness, and is thus
'almost male', and a male of the cerebral sort. Conventional
readers were prepared to be shocked by *Jude*, and it appears
that they consented to be shocked without analysing the
occasion. 'Morbid', 'warped and neurotic' were terms applied
by the more observant reviewers (see Cox, 1970, p. 295); the
anonymous reviewer in the *Illustrated London News* is more
typical of the stock impression: Sue suffers 'from the too
evident effort to focus in her all the restless imaginings of our
modern adventurous womanhood' (Cox, 1970, p. 276). Those
who recognize that Sue's restless imaginings bring her little

pleasure, even in the shortest term, are more inclined to accuse her of flirtation than to understand, let alone sympathize with her. Having labelled Arabella 'a human pig', and much more, Mrs Oliphant passed on to Sue, who 'completes the circle of the unclean':

> ...the fleshly animal Arabella and the fantastic Susan, the one ready to gratify him in whatever circumstances they may meet, the other holding him on the tiptoe of expectation, with a pretended reserve which is almost more indecent still.

> (Cox, 1970, p. 258)

That 'pretended reserve' shocks; it assumes knowledge, and denies Sue's problem, as it denies the problem of Sue.

Lawrence's contribution to the understanding of Hardy's characters has been either ignored or dismissed as obviously wrong-headed. By the time the contemporary feminist debate began to take *Jude* for one of its central texts, the stereotypes had been inverted. By 1969, when Kate Millett wrote of *Jude* in *Sexual Politics*, it was assumed that Hardy was on the side of the feminists, and therefore that something had gone strangely wrong with the presentation of Sue:

> *Jude the Obscure* is on very solid ground when attacking the class system, but when it turns to the sexual revolution, Hardy himself is troubled and confused.

> (Millett, 1969, pp. 133-4)

The wonder here is that there *ought* to be a feminist stereotype, and that Hardy is to be faulted for not conforming. Millett's charge was well answered by Mary Jacobus in an essay, 'Sue the Obscure' (1975), that argued for the deliberate uncertainty and 'obscurity' of Hardy's characterization of Sue. Lawrence, however, has subsequently been little called upon, and then, sometimes, belittlingly, as by John Goode: 'Lawrence's later reading of Arabella as some kind of natural energy only shows that he was as vulnerable to barmaids as the rest of us' (Goode, 1988, p. 149).

The embarrassment of this put-down may reveal something of the desperation with which we stick to stereotypes. There is, after all, no more justification in speaking of Arabella by generalizing about barmaids than in the reduction of Jude to a generic stonemason, or Tess to a generic dairymaid. So obviously are the novels concerned with not conflating person with trade or occupation, that even an unsympathetic reader is likely to find Arabella rather vividly individual. And the sheer impossibility of describing Sue in generic terms (the typical schoolteacher?) suggests Hardy's deliberate intent to keep her obscurely herself.

We might expect a greater sensitivity to these matters to be displayed by Virginia Woolf. In her essay 'The Novels of Thomas Hardy', written on the occasion of his death in January 1928, and published in *The Second Common Reader* (1932), we find no discussion at all of the question of the sexes, and some unease with *Jude the Obscure*. It may be worth pointing out also that Hardy is not mentioned in *A Room of One's Own*, published in 1929. Far from seeing Hardy as engaged in ideological struggle, specifically the struggle over the representation of women, Woolf – as we have already seen – endorses the notion of Hardy as somnambulist:

> Some, like Henry James and Flaubert, are able not merely to make the best use of the spoil their gifts bring in, but control their genius in the act of creation; they are aware of all the possibilities of every situation, and are never taken by surprise. The unconscious writers, on the other hand, like Dickens and Scott, seem suddenly and without their own consent to be lifted up and swept onwards.... Among them – it is the source of his strength and of his weakness – we must place Hardy.... The novels therefore are full of inequalities; they are lumpish and dull and inexpressive; but they are never arid; there is always about them a little blur of unconsciousness, that halo of freshness and margin of the unexpressed which often produce the most profound sense of satisfaction. It is as if Hardy himself were not quite aware of

what he did, as if his consciousness held more than he could produce....

(Woolf, 1932, pp. 188-9)

Hardy has been so often associated with this notion of 'unconsciousness' that one might suspect therein a device to avoid, apologize for, or legitimately overlook, the conscious, deliberate ideological theme of the novels. With James or Flaubert, according to this division, we cannot read in the text anything that has not been purposefully put there, and we therefore cannot ignore anything in the text that we have seen. In Dickens, Scott or Hardy, however, we can find all sorts of things that the author did not intend, and therefore we can lightly disregard some elements that the author may have intended.

Woolf manages, at any rate, to render Hardy free of ideological impurities. A potentially interesting discussion of Hardy's characters observes how little we know, or recall, about how two characters met and fell in love, but that we do have a very strong impression of emotions and passions as 'great facts' (Woolf, 1932, p. 192). In consequence we know Hardy's characters as subjects or victims of passions, rather than as autonomous human beings.

We do not remember how they talked and changed and got to know each other, finely, gradually.... Their relationship is not composed of those intellectual apprehensions and subtleties of perception which seem so slight yet are so profound.... The talk between the lovers when it is not passionate is practical or philosophic, as though the discharge of their daily duties left them with more desire to question life and its purpose than to investigate each other's sensibilities....

There is in the work of the great classical writers a finality of effect which places certain of their scenes...beyond the reach of change.... A laugh, a blush, half a dozen words of dialogue, and it is enough; the source of our delight is perennial. But Hardy has none of this concentration and completeness. His light does not fall directly upon the human heart. It passes over it and out on to the darkness of the heath.... Each man or woman is battling with the storm, alone, revealing himself most when he is least under the observation of other human beings. We do not know them as we know Pierre or Natasha or Becky Sharp. We do not know them in and out and all round as they are revealed to the casual caller, to the Government official, to the great lady, to the general on the battlefield. We do not know the complication and involvement and turmoil of their thoughts.

(Woolf, 1932, pp. 192-3)

This accords well with Lawrence's observations, and suggests that Hardy should be given credit for undoing 'the old stable ego' of traditional fiction, and thus for making possible the fiction of Lawrence, Woolf and other modernists. Yet, perhaps characteristically, Woolf compensates for creative experimentation with critical nostalgia. Jane Austen, Tolstoy and Thackeray represent the classical novel that Woolf was not interested in following, and it ought therefore to be precisely Hardy's distinction that he does not presume to that lofty, comprehensive knowledge of humanity which is the pride and prerogative of 'the great novelists'.

Hardy's readings in contemporary philosophy and science no doubt contributed to his devising a presentation of fictional character that did not subscribe to individualistic theories of the subject. Novels may be written out of a sense of the inadequacy of previous novels; Hardy's characters may be attributed, then, not to Hardy's 'unconsciousness' but to his dissatisfaction with unified, coherent and thoroughly comprehended characters in 'traditional' fiction. As Deleuze draws on Lawrence's account of Hardy, so he might have drawn on Woolf's paragraph cited above. But that paragraph continues, if such a hiatus can be called a continuation, and retracts:

We do not know the complication and involvement and turmoil of their thoughts. Geographically, too, they remain fixed to the same stretch of the English country-side. It is seldom, and always with unhappy results, that Hardy leaves the yeoman or farmer to describe the class above theirs in the social scale. In the drawing-room and clubroom and ballroom, where people of leisure and education come together, where comedy is bred and shades of character revealed, he is awkward and ill at ease. But the opposite is equally true. If we do not know his men and women in their relationships to each other, we know them in their relationships to time, death, and fate.

After seven more sentences, the paragraph reaches its conclusion:

They have a force in them which cannot be defined, a force of love or of hate, a force which in the men is the cause of rebellion against life, and in the women implies an illimitable capacity for suffering, and it is this which dominates the character and makes it unnecessary that we should see the finer features that lie hid. This is the tragic power; and, if we are to place Hardy among his fellows, we must call him the greatest tragic writer among English novelists.

(Woolf, 1932, pp. 192-3)

The movement of the paragraph can be described as an uncovering of how Hardy differs from all other novelists, followed by a refusal to pursue the implications, and a covering up with the safe stereotypes of the English countryside and tragedy. Classification by genre can always be reductive, and the ascription of a work of literature to the class of 'Tragedy' is condescending if undeserved, or, if deserved, a sly domestication (see Mizener, 1940; Kramer, 1975).

Seven pages have brought Virginia Woolf to the brink of something interesting, and carried her safely away again. That she herself recognizes this may be clear from the opening of the next paragraph with its metaphor of scout and sapper:

But let us, as we approach the danger-zone of Hardy's philos-

ophy, be on our guard. Nothing is more necessary, in reading
an imaginative writer, than to keep at the right distance
above his page. Nothing is easier, especially with a writer of
marked idiosyncrasy, than to fasten on opinions, convict him
of a creed, tether him to a consistent point of view. Nor was
Hardy any exception to the rule that the mind which is most
capable of receiving impressions is very often the least capable of drawing conclusions. It is for the reader, steeped in
the impression, to supply the comment. It is his part to know
when to put aside the writer's conscious intention in favour
of some deeper intention of which perhaps he may be unconscious. Hardy himself was aware of this.

(Woolf, 1932, p. 193)

The confusion, double-thought and double standards here
are properly disturbing. The reader is licensed to make of a
great text virtually what she will; Woolf, after all, has been
granted privileged access to the author's deeper intention,
and even knows that the author recognizes his helplessness
and argumentative incompetence. Evidence of this latter, of
the author's abject concession of authority to the reader, is
taken from Hardy's litotic and self-deprecating prefaces:

A novel 'is an impression, not an argument,' he has warned
us.... Certainly it is true to say of him that, at his greatest,
he gives us impressions; at his weakest, arguments. In *The
Woodlanders, The Return of the Native, Far from the Madding
Crowd*, and, above all, in *The Mayor of Casterbridge*, we have
Hardy's impression of life as it came to him without conscious
ordering. Let him once begin to tamper with his direct intui-
tions and his power is gone....

(Woolf, 1932, pp. 193-4)

One marvels that a practising novelist should be able to write
of a fellow-artist, or of a fellow-craftsman, in such terms as
these. It would be inexplicable, were it not in the service of
ideological mine-sweeping:

That is the reason why *Jude the Obscure* is the most painful of all Hardy's books, and the only one against which we can fairly bring the charge of pessimism. In *Jude the Obscure* argument is allowed to dominate impression, with the result that though the misery of the book is overwhelming it is not tragic.

(Woolf, 1932, p. 194)

Jude's offence may lie very simply in the fact that it resists classification; Woolf's offence is that she allows a number of odd and awkward and ill-fitting elements of the book to constitute a 'charge' against it.

The reason why *Jude the Obscure* is not tragic, for Woolf as for Lawrence, is that Hardy has picked his quarrel not with the gods but with the forms of social organization, and in his argument he has loaded the scales:

As calamity succeeds calamity we feel that the case against society is not being argued fairly or with profound understanding of the facts. Here is nothing of that width and force and knowledge of mankind which, when Tolstoy criticises society, makes his indictment formidable. Here we have revealed to us the petty cruelty of man, not the large injustice of the gods. It is only necessary to compare *Jude the Obscure* with *The Mayor of Casterbridge* to see where Hardy's true power lay. Jude carries on his miserable contest against the deans of colleges and the conventions of sophisticated society. Henchard is pitted, not against another man, but against something outside himself which is opposed to men of his ambition and power.

(Woolf, 1932, p. 194)

The 'petty cruelty of men' and Jude's 'miserable contest' have the effect of justifying the social, institutional, 'man-made' status quo. Who are 'the gods', what is this 'something outside himself', against which the true tragic hero is 'pitted'? It may be that Hardy is writing a critique of tragedy, precisely to point out its conservative role in blaming what can be neither identified nor prevented, and in exonerating the existent, the actual and the amendable. Hardy's reference to 'the gods' 'in Aeschylean phrase' at the close of *Tess* would lose all its force if it were taken literally, if one assumed the narrator or author to have any such belief. To take the phrase ironically does not help much either, for then we would have the tragic gesture in full awareness of the absence of the necessary metaphysic. The close of *Jude* is overwhelmingly miserable because there is no metaphysical escape clause, even of an ironic kind.

As Marxism confers on 'History' a quasi-transcendental status (at least), it can, when appropriate or expedient, exonerate the ruling-class for not knowing what it is about. Feminism, as a form of social critique, is much more direct and unforgiving in its attribution of responsibility. Marxism addresses the human condition, finds it wanting and attempts to ameliorate it. Precisely in its refusal to recognize 'the human condition' feminism locates all oppression and misery – everything that made that 'condition' less than desirable – in the deliberate organization of society by those who benefit from it. The attraction of feminist critics (including Kate Millett and others outside the profession of literary criticism) to *Jude the Obscure* may be best explained not by the themes of that novel, nor by its characterizations of women, but simply by its astonishingly unprecedented refusal to shift blame to a quasi-transcendental plane. Why then should Virginia Woolf, whose *Room of One's Own* has become a canonical text of feminist literary criticism, have worked so earnestly and, as we have seen, so unreasonably, to exclude Hardy, to deny that he made common cause with her endeavours? One has only to survey a range of works of general feminist literary criticism, and a range of feminist criticism of the novels of Hardy, to note this disparity: in the former Woolf is cited regularly and almost ritually, while in the latter her name is seldom even mentioned.

Explanations could be proposed in terms of the tension in Woolf between the claims of radicalism and of Bloomsbury, or of the conflict with her father: between Leslie Stephen as

Hardy's editor and mentor, and Leslie Stephen as Mr Ramsay in *To the Lighthouse*. One could also point out that Woolf's criticism is anyway at odds with her fiction, given that her fiction is likely to prove somewhat difficult for the 'common reader' celebrated in the two volumes of collected critical essays. However, rather than explain the anomaly with reference to Woolf's biography, it might be more revealing to treat it as symptomatic of the uncertain position, not only of Hardy's reputation, but of his position within or outside literary traditions and movements.

During the era of High Modernism (roughly 1910-30) there was what might be called a selective acknowledgement and appreciation of precursors. The opposition – what was to be overthrown – was familiar, conventional and invariably English. The new, the exotic, the alien was inevitably foreign. Thus one finds Eliot celebrating Laforgue, Joyce celebrating Dujardin and Ibsen, not because these foreign writers are more revolutionary and experimental than any writers in the English language, but because they have the rhetorical function of being alien. Truly experimental foreign writers such as Mallarmé or Pirandello or Unamuno play an insignificant part in English Modernism. The immediate precursors of Modernism tended to get labelled 'Victorian' and that label of course applied only to English writers. We have no term with which to express our (now conventional) disdain for old-fashioned foreigners such as Hugo, Manzoni and Sienkiewicz. And one cannot *épater les bourgeoises* while speaking English.

The result of this (which probably owes as much to Edward VII as to any intellectual or aesthetic programme) is that we have established a hiatus where there might be continuity; and that hiatus between 'Victorian' and 'Modernist' is maintained only by a ruthless application of the law of the excluded middle. Hardy has been firmly placed on the Victorian side of the abyss. In one way, of course, this was an inevitable consequence of the 'Wessex Edition' with its sepia-toned frontispieces – reassuringly familiar volumes in 1912; at a time when, according to Woolf, human nature had recently been altered. And there was a need for reassurance and familiarity, even, one might suppose, among the avant-garde. Woolf writes about Miss Mitford and Parson Woodforde, and those essays are of a piece with her description of Hardy's prose 'like Dorsetshire itself' (Woolf, 1932, p. 195).

How deeply comforting it must have been, amidst the later anxieties of 1942, to hear Lord David Cecil's Clark Lectures at Cambridge, or to read, in 1943, *Hardy the Novelist*:

> Hardy was a man born after his time – the last lonely representative of an ancient race, strayed, by some accident of Destiny, into the alien world of the later nineteenth century.... The society in which he was brought up was that in which the ancient mode of life lingered longest. Rural Wessex was still feudal pre-industrial Wessex, with its villages clustering round the great houses and church, with its long-established families and time-hallowed customs, its whole habit of mind moulded by the tradition of the past.... He was the typical child of such a society – simple, unselfconscious, passionate, instinctively turning for his imaginative nourishment to the fundamental drama and comedy of human life, responsive to the basic joys and sorrows of mankind, to the love of home, to the beauty of spring and sunshine, the charm of innocence; to fun and conviviality and the grandeur of heroism; to the horror of death and the terrors of superstition. His talent was of a piece with the rest of him – naive and epic, massive and careless, quaint and majestic, ignorant of the niceties of craft, delighting shamelessly in a sensational tale, but able to rise to the boldest flights of imagination. So far from being the first of the modern school of novelists, Hardy is the last representative of the tradition and spirit of the Elizabethan drama.

(Cecil, 1943, pp. 148-9)

It is easy to make light of this now, but we should not do so without recognizing how much, and how deeply, Hardy criticism is implicated in Lord David Cecil's epitome (see Widdowson, 1989, pp. 24-6). Hardy evokes a world that we have lost in all but his novels, and Shakespeare's pastoral comedies, and landscape paintings. Cecil does not pretend that that world is immutable; he recognizes the sense of loss, and its force: 'It is still the Elizabethan world, but the Elizabethan world with the lights going down; and gathering round it the dusk that heralds its final oblivion' (Cecil, 1943, p. 149).

Hardy thus became emblematic of a double loss: of the loss of a simpler world, agricultural, chronicled by the seasons, in which feelings are forthright and strong, and lives harsh but honourable. And of the loss of a simpler aesthetic; for the representation of such a world had appeal to the general public regardless of educational attainments. The ideal of 'the common reader' brings together Woolf, Eliot and the Leavises, and is almost always the instrument of a conservative criticism: whether the present malaise is due to industrialization, or television, or the dissociation of sensibility, it is clear that there was once a better age than ours. Simplicity has a clear ethical value, and an increase in complexity signifies decline. Hardy's 'unconsciousness' carries the ideological value of an Arcadian or prelapsarian age in which there was no labour. The absence of struggle and effort is indicated further by Cecil's attribution to Hardy's works of naiveté:

> He was a simple man – how often have I found myself using the word 'naive' in these lectures.... He reacts to experience, both sad and happy, with the unquestioning whole-heartedness of a child.
>
> (Cecil, 1943, pp. 153-4)

This, coming at the end of the Clark lectures, provides the conclusion to one of Cecil's early claims, that Hardy was 'aesthetically...a man of the past...much more like...Fielding than...Henry James' (Cecil, 1943, p. 39).

The complexity of the modern age, and the necessary difficulty of its aesthetic representations – as Eliot argued – thereby reinforce each other's decline. Hardy represents in simple manner a simple society, and those who are opposed to both modernity and modernism can find much solace therein. However, what Hardy represents politically is not simple at all. The same perspective that affords nostalgia for conservatives also provides a mode of critique for socialist critics unhappy with the specifics of modernity rather than with the phenomenon itself. There is an obvious continuity between the lament of Lord David Cecil and that of Douglas Brown in 1954, however offensive that may sound to those subsequent critics who cite Brown respectfully and frequently, and whose mentions of Cecil are confined to the dismissive (e.g., Kettle 1966: a Marxist work that praises Brown but has the very tone and cadence of Cecil: 'grounded in centuries of custom…the age-old festivals', etc.). Brown's thesis is that the countryside is good, the town evil. This leads Brown to such claims as that 'the lowlands' of the poem 'Wessex Heights' stands for 'the urban environment' (Brown, 1954, p. 164) and that Tess undergoes two 'restorations': once at Talbothays, and once at Flintcomb Ash. The catastrophe, according to Brown, occurs not in the Chase, for that is far too unspoilt and pre-industrial to be the site of evil, but in 'Budmouth' (Brown, 1954, p. 93). (His hatred of towns is so intense that Budmouth and Sandbourne amount to much the same thing.) Brown's general contention is that: 'each of the great Wessex novels treats in imaginative form of the defeat of our peasantry and the collapse of our agriculture' (Brown, 1954, p. 36). Even Lord David Cecil does not attain to the aristocratic aplomb of that phrase: 'our peasantry.'

Concern for our peasantry has activated much socially aware criticism of the past 30 years, in particular the influential work of Raymond Williams. Both in *The English Novel from Dickens to Lawrence* and in *The Country and the City*, Williams sees Hardy as advocating the values of rural community against urban industrial society – *gemeinschaft* versus *Gesellschaft*. For Williams, London society is 'a world Hardy should never have got near; never have let himself be exposed to' (Williams, 1973, p. 199). Reading Brown, Kettle and Williams, one begins to understand who is being addressed so insistently by Hardy in his ghosted (auto)biography when he lists every lord and lady that he ever shared a reception room with. Williams certainly improves on the detail of Brown's thesis, most basically by observing the obvious – that there was in the Dorset of Hardy's time no such thing as a peasant class. He goes on to describe the tension in Hardy's work between the one who is immersed in rural society, who knows its ways intimately, and the writer whose education and career have removed him from his home, have made his former intimacy an uncertainty of distance and viewpoint (Williams, 1973, p. 200). The title of Williams' chapter is 'Wessex and the Border', and this is explained:

> ...the real Hardy country...is that border country so many of us have been living in: between custom and education, be-tween work and ideas, between love of place and an exper-ience of change.

> (Williams, 1973, p. 197)

Williams, in other words, reads Hardy in the light of his own novel of 1960, *Border Country*, and thus imposes on Hardy his own constant tension between the demands of radicalism and the lure of nostalgia. Williams' reading of Hardy might be more productive at a biographical level than it is convinc-ing as a critical device; even here, however, there is little evidence of Hardy suffering that particular tension, unless the absence be the evidence – as it is for such a biographer as Robert Gittings.

Radical criticism has taken a long time to free itself from the ambivalence of Williams' influence and prestige. George Wotton's *Thomas Hardy: Towards a Materialist Criticism* (1985) tactfully establishes a distance, and recent works by John Goode and Peter Widdowson have broken with the rural–radical syndrome by attending to the social satire of such novels as *The Hand of Ethelberta*.

An anonymous review of Douglas Brown's *Thomas Hardy* makes this observation:

> Mr. Brown starts with a remarkable decision. Because he thinks that the claims of *The Dynasts* as a work of literature

are relatively slight, he has left it aside altogether. Had he been writing a book merely about the novels and short stories this would have been acceptable. But his theme is Thomas Hardy. As it is, some of his most percipient pages are...about the poems. Thomas Hardy cannot be considered as a whole without *The Dynasts*.

(*The Times*, May 1954)

Edmund Blunden's identically titled *Thomas Hardy* of 1942 had given comprehensive treatment to all aspects of Hardy's work: Cecil's decisive image of Hardy as eulogist and elegist of the Wessex countryside was put forward in *Hardy the Novelist*. That restrictive and respectful modifier has seldom been found necessary by later writers. But it is not only *The Dynasts* that is omitted from general and apparently comprehensive studies of Thomas Hardy; *The Hand of Ethelberta*, *A Laodicean* and the other 'minor novels' fade from view. Hardy's choice of 'Wessex' as descriptive of his collected works seems to have provided authorial warrant for the reduction of Hardy's range and a narrowing of the critical focus. It is a triumph of documentary realism that, whether it serves the nostalgia for pre-modernity or the critique of the modernity we have, Hardy becomes an instrument of ideological gratification.

One is tempted to suggest that the outbreak of the Second World War served as a fixative on the distant view of Wessex; not only did the experience of war make readers turn to fiction for images of security, but English rural society itself was fundamentally affected by the wartime mechanization of agriculture, almost as drastic as industrialism in its effect of depopulating the countryside. In 1941 Edmund Blunden completed his monograph on Hardy, and concluded his preface with a tribute to his subject 'whose memory...shines steadily through all decline and change' (Blunden, 1942, p. viii). One can sense the lack of conviction with which Blunden attempts to mock the wistful mood evoked by a photograph:

The 1908 edition of Wilkinson Sherren's *The Wessex of Romance* contained a picture of Hardy the cyclist, standing in a
lane with his machine, check knickerbockers and panama
hat: great days!

(Blunden, 1942, p. 117)

That pervasive tone belies the depth and quality of Blunden's
research, notably into the early reviews of Hardy's work.
Blunden is the first to cite William Archer's review of *Wessex
Poems* with its astute observation in reference to 'The Peasant's Confession', that Hardy seemed

to lose all sense of local and historical perspective in language,
seeing all the words in the dictionary on one plane, so to
speak, and regarding them all as equally available and appropriate for any and every literary purpose.

(Blunden, 1942, p. 104; for Elliott, 1984, p. 196,
this is a 'now-familiar comment', although
never cited before 1942, and seldom since)

Blunden also gives an extract from Hardy's letter to Archer:
'Concluding that the tale must be regarded as a translation
of the original utterance of the peasant, I thought an impersonal wording admissible.' Recent publication of that letter,
dated 21 December 1898, shows Blunden selecting Hardy's
words to give a defensive tone. What actually precedes that
extract transforms the tone:

Your happy phrase, 'seeing all the words of the dictionary on
one plane'...touches, curiously enough, what I had thought
over.

(Purdy and Millgate, 1978-88, ii, p. 207)

That undefensive endorsement of a reviewer's insight may
have been omitted not because Blunden wants to display
Hardy's 'morbid sensitivity' to reviews (his presentation of

Hardy is among the most urbane and self-possessed) but, rather, because it reveals too much of Hardy's conscious control over his text. We see Blunden's problem in the ambivalence of his way of praising the language of *The Dynasts*, praise that follows or modifies Archer's enthusiasm for 'The Peasant's Confession':

> For the whole production is, and it must have been, characterized and completed in its nature by an innovation of word-choice. The two aspects of life which Hardy intends to portray and interpret are the tangible and the spectral, or the real and the phantasmal. The types of words which he wants for his principle utterances are thus the local, graphic, primitive, hard, and the psychological, subtle, abstract – between which two, in the progress of his theme, he may sometimes discover, recreate or compel a surprising relationship.

> (Blunden, 1942, p. 236)

'Discover, recreate or compel' pulls back somewhat from the decisive intention implied by 'word-choice'. Yet Blunden's sense that Hardy's linguistic effects are not happy accidents has pointed the way to recent studies by Ralph W.V. Elliott and Raymond Chapman – studies liberated by the confidence that Hardy knew, linguistically and stylistically, what he was about.

That Blunden was himself a poet is, of course, significant, for one can detect a pattern in which it is the appreciation of Hardy's poetry by poets that leads to greater attentiveness to the formal qualities of Hardy's fiction. While Blunden's contribution was muffled by his rather antiquated and whimsical manner, itself consonant with wartime and the sense of social and historical discontinuities, other poets could speak more clearly. In the United States criticism was, at its independent best, free of the burdens of nostalgia, social history, and regionalism. Those freedoms are richly exemplified in the special centenary issue of *The Southern Review*, published in 1940 when the centenary of Hardy's birth could be barely acknowledged in Britain. Of the volume's fourteen essays, eight are devoted entirely to the poetry of Hardy; the distinction of the contributors has ensured that this volume remains the starting-point for any critical consideration of Hardy's poetry.

In 1940 Hardy's poetry was highly regarded, in part because Hardy had asked throughout the last 30 years of his life that it should be valued more than his fiction; this insistence found posthumous force in Hardy's disguised autobiography. The continuing assumption that true literary greatness was properly poetic encouraged a fairly uncritical admiration of Hardy's poetry. When that admiration was spelt out, which was seldom, it was in terms of Hardy's ideas and wisdom: Hardy, being a great poet, was spoken about as one would speak of other great poets. (Two particularly fine early essays are by G. R. Elliott, 1928.) *The Dynasts* was central, and those poems close to its themes and concerns were given prominence; Matthew Arnold was regularly cited for comparison. Even I.A. Richards in an early book, *Science and Poetry* (1926), singles Hardy out for reflecting the intellectual movements of his age: he is 'the poet who has most fully and courageously accepted the contemporary background' (Richards, 1926, p. 68). Richards builds on Middleton Murry's view of Hardy as a poetic sage (Murry, 1920), and modifies it by playing down what he calls Hardy's 'short essays in verse' in favour of four poems now extremely familiar: 'The Self-Unseeing', 'The Voice', 'A Broken Appointment' and 'After a Journey'.

F. R. Leavis, in *New Bearings in English Poetry* (1932), accepted Richards' account of Hardy but ignored his deprecation of the 'short essays in verse'. For Leavis this merely showed how Hardy's reputation as a poet rested on nonpoetic circumstances, and that the application of critical standards would reveal how little of his poetry was really distinguished. Leavis also makes use of the critical tradition that Hardy wrote spontaneously and unconsciously, relying on the (most unreliable) testimony of Robert Graves in *Goodbye To All That*: 'Why!', he said, 'I have never in my life taken more than three, or perhaps four drafts for a poem. I am afraid of it losing its freshness' (Leavis, 1932, p. 48; Graves,

1929, p. 249). To this excerpt Leavis adds the comment: 'It is all in keeping with this precritical innocence that his great poems should be only a very small proportion of his abundant output' (Leavis, 1932, p. 48). He lists six of the dozen great poems of Hardy: the four given by Richards, plus 'Neutral Tones' and 'During Wind and Rain'. Leavis then asserts that the 'great poems' (these and a further unspecified six) are never represented in anthologies, and that his purpose is to rescue the poems that matter, and to prevent the collapse of Hardy's poetic reputation as his comments and ideas cease to be of moment.

In 1940 Leavis was asked to contribute to *The Southern Review*, on Hardy's poetry, and he begins by letting it be known what he thinks of the novels (some eight years before *The Great Tradition*):

> When *The Southern Review* honoured me with the invitation to contribute to this centennial issue I replied with the warning that I didn't share the generally accepted estimate of Hardy. I think, in fact, that it greatly overexalts him. I used once to say that I shouldn't have known he was a great novelist if I hadn't been told. After sufficiently dogged attempts to arrive at a less dissident valuation I am now convinced that he is not one...the justice that I am convinced ought to be done is not merely a matter of deprivation: Hardy stands to gain by it – if, that is, I am right in my belief that his acceptance as a poet is almost wholly conventional. For though I shouldn't think of calling Hardy a great poet, I do believe that he wrote a certain amount of major poetry. And this major poetry is hardly ever represented in anthologies that bring him in.

> (Leavis, 1940, p. 87)

Leavis exaggerates both the general enthusiasm for the bulk of Hardy's poetry, and the anthologists' neglect of what he regards as 'major' (see Johnson, 1979). Leavis is prepared to discuss, with a tolerance bordering on approval, more poems in 1940 than he had in 1932. 'Friends Beyond', 'Julie-Jane',

'The Darkling Thrush', 'Shut Out That Moon' and 'The Night of the Dance' deserve 'to be handed down; poems that present in quintessential form what is most living in the novels' (Leavis, 1940, p. 91). Which is odd praise given Leavis' valuation of the novels. But the number of poems that can be considered 'major' has now been halved, from the dozen of which six were named in 1932, to those six alone. Such details may belong in a pathology of critical taste and polemic. But Leavis' readings of 'The Voice' and 'After a Journey' were refreshingly stringent, and eased six major poems into the canon of the New Critics.

Leavis' ambivalence about Hardy is revealed in the oddity of both his praise and dispraise, which are not always readily distinguishable. This may be because everything that is bad in Hardy very occasionally becomes 'transmuted' into poetic virtue. This is Leavis praising 'The Voice':

> The first stanza might seem to threaten one of those crude popular lilts which Hardy is so fond of.... Actually, the bare prosaic stating manner, which elsewhere would have been Hardy's characteristic gaucherie, turns the lilt into a subtle movement...the shift of stress on the rhyme ('viéw you then,' 'knew you thén') has banished all danger of jingle. In the third stanza we have one of those Hardy coinages, 'existlessness'. In itself it might seem a typically awkward eccentricity, yet as it comes here it is peculiarly right, conveying vacancy in the sough of the breeze. Later Hardy changed it for 'wan wistlessness', which is now current as the final reading – he was not, one feels, an artist whose successes were associated with a refined critical consciousness. Yet it is an exquisite sureness of touch – hardly suggesting a naif artist – that is manifested in the changed movement of the last stanza, with its effect as of a subsiding into the recognition of utter loss.

> (Leavis, 1940, p. 93; expanded version of Leavis, 1932, pp. 48-9)

In *The Southern Review* Leavis was not only more expansive and tolerant over a range of Hardy's poems, but he was prepared to go beyond innuendo in explaining what was wrong with most of Hardy's poetry. The use of paradox and oxymoron may indicate how close failure and success can be:

> In saying that his characteristic verse has no distinction one is not intending to deny that it is characteristic: it is positively, even aggressively, so. Lack of distinction in Hardy becomes a positive quality. If one says that he seems to have no sensitiveness for words, one recognizes at the same time that he has made a style out of stylelessness. There is something extremely personal about the gauche unshrinking mismarriages – group mismarriages – of his diction, in which, with naif aplomb, he takes as they come the romantic-poetical, the prosaic banal, the stilted literary, the colloquial, the archaistic, the erudite, the technical, the dialect word, the brand-new Hardy coinage.

> (Leavis, 1940, p. 92)

That is what Archer had noticed about the diction of 'The Peasant's Confession' being all on one plane, and it is by no means obvious that this is a bad thing. As Leavis finds things to praise, he finds them very often in the transmuting of what is otherwise characteristic and gauche. Leavis' argument against the mass of Hardy's poems is flimsy, and falls far short of justifying his patronizing pronouncements.

In initiating the American critical debate about Hardy as a poet, Richards and Leavis had excluded from the discussion (Leavis, as we have seen, more rigorously than Richards) everything that would fix Hardy in his time and nation. What was left was a Hardy consonant with the predilections and needs of those tendencies in American academic criticism that would define themselves as the New Criticism. The essays in *The Southern Review* by John Crowe Ransom, R.P. Blackmur, Delmore Schwartz and Allen Tate exemplify the New Criticism at its least dogmatic, and they remain among the finest contributions to the criticism of Hardy's poetry. All but Blackmur of the four were poets themselves, and Ransom especially pays practitioner's attention to Hardy's metres:

No poet has a firmer sense of the function of the meter than
Hardy has. I think of him as a poet who strains to make his
meters without impairing his sense, and in straining succeeds. The signs of strain look like an honest effort, and I
dislike to put a more unfavourable construction upon this
aspect.

(Ransom, 1940, p. 12)

Following the Leavis doctrine, however, Ransom qualifies his
praise by summing Hardy up as 'a great minor poet...and a
poor major poet' (Ransom, 1940, p. 14). Blackmur (than
whom few critics have ever been more truly independent)
takes up Leavis' assumption of Hardy's precritical innocence
and its unconscious successes – which probably derives from
Virginia Woolf – and worries it with magnificent discernment
and persistence: 'The theory of accidents in poetry like that
of idiopathy in medicine is only a cloak for inadequate observation and explains nothing' (Blackmur, 1940, p. 26). Dis-
cussing these lines from 'She to Him III':

Numb as a vane that cankers on its point,
True to the wind that kissed ere canker came...

Blackmur celebrates Hardy's absorption of tradition:

It is the tradition not only at work, but met, and used.
Doubtless Hardy had read a good deal of Elizabethan and
Jacobean poetry, and got from his reading the themes as well
as the means of his early poems; certainly in this poem, for
two lines, he got the full authority of the form at once as a
cumulus and as a fresh instance. Authority, then, is the word
of explanation that we wanted, and we may take it in two
senses: the principle of derived right and as the very quality
of authorship which has as its perfection the peculiar objective virtue of anonymity. That is one's gain from tradition:
anonymous authority....
    Meanwhile it is a good deal of weight to heap on two lines;
the pity is that it cannot be generally heaped over the whole

body of Hardy's verse. That is the privative fact about most of Hardy's verse: he dispensed with tradition in most of his ambitious verse; it is willful where it should be authoritative, idiosyncratic where it should be anonymous.... It is so by choice, but not exactly by discrimination; rather choice by a series of those chances to whose operation in the moral field Hardy was so warmly addicted.

(Blackmur, 1940, p. 27)

Even Blackmur defers to the reservations of the advanced British critics about Hardy's stature, and repeats the platitudes about his ideas attempting to be a substitute for poetic craft: 'what Hardy really lacked was the craft of his profession'(Blackmur, 1940, p. 28). Blackmur's allegiance to this conventional view forces him to venture a paradox that makes little sense:

In Hardy's case, the interesting fact is that he sometimes possessed the tradition and sometimes did not; and the fertile possibility is that possession or lack may explain what otherwise seems the accident of success or failure.

(Blackmur, 1940, p. 29)

Hardy is still being denied the consciousness wherewith he could determine for himself the extent and quality of tradition to be deployed.

Alluding then to Leavis' paradox of Hardy making a style out of stylelessness, Blackmur poses another paradox: he takes the conventional understanding of 'style' to be the antithesis of anonymous authority. The latter quality Blackmur finds in abundance in the 'Poems of 1912-13' now, but not then, universally acknowledged as among Hardy's greatest. Blackmur is the first critic to celebrate these poems, poems

...so strong that all that was personal – the private drive, the private grief – is cut away and the impersonal is left bare, an old monument, mutilated or weathered as you like to call it,

of that face which the personal only hides.... Like the others
in the series, ['The Walk'] is a poem almost without style; it
is style reduced to anonymity, reduced to riches....

(Blackmur, 1940, p. 47)

That anonymity and authority are threatened when Hardy
relies not on his emotions and his memory, but depends
instead on ideas. T.S. Eliot said of Henry James that his was
a mind so refined that it could not be violated by ideas. The
comparison between Hardy and James is thus implied by
Blackmur in his cautiously qualified conclusion:

Hardy is the great example of a sensibility violated by ideas;
and perhaps the unique example, since Swift, of the sensibility great enough...to survive the violation.

(Blackmur, 1940, p. 48)

One is struck throughout *The Southern Review*, by the resistance to large claims, the niggardliness of praise, the note of
apology that at once declares and forswears enthusiasm.
Hardy is still the uneducated countryman, but one feels it as
a relief when this is, for once, held against him, as if it
obscured his true importance. New Criticism was utterly
opposed to the complex of nostalgia, social history and topography connoted by 'Wessex' and, with Hardy as with other
writers, it turned to advantage the American distance from,
or lack of, the mimetic referent of English literature.

Entirely fitting, then, that the most famous essay in the
summer 1940, issue of *The Southern Review* was one of the
earliest pieces written by W.H. Auden in the United States.
Its title, 'Literary Transference', alludes to the movement of
Auden's poetic enthusiasm from Hardy to Eliot, and equally
to the crossings in Auden's own life. We note in Auden's
reminiscences how closely, for all his claims of an old-fashioned childhood and isolated adolescence, his view of
Hardy matches I.A. Richards' view of Hardy as poet and as
exemplar of intellectual developments, and that both views

were held in the years 1923-6:

> ...Hardy in the summer of 1923; for more than a year I read
> no one else, and I do not think that I was ever without one
> volume or another of the beautifully produced Wessex edition
> in my hands: I smuggled them into class.... In the autumn of
> 1924 there was a palace revolution after which he had to share
> his kingdom with Edward Thomas, until finally they were
> both defeated by Eliot at the battle of Oxford in 1926.
>
> Besides serving as the archetype of the Poetic, Hardy was
> also an expression of the Contemporary Scene. He was both
> my Keats and my Carl Sandburg.

> (Auden, 1940, p. 80)

Auden's essay opens startlingly: 'I cannot write objectively
about Thomas Hardy because I was once in love with him',
and the real difficulty lies in explaining how that love ended.
In a passage even more distractingly Jungian than the rest
of the essay, Auden tells us that Hardy looked like his own
father, and that he, Auden, as a thinking-intuitive, took after
his mother. Having told us that Hardy's 'direct colloquial
diction' was 'more fertile and adaptable to different themes
than any of Eliot's gas-works and rats' feet', Auden is hard
put to explain why he transferred his poetic allegiance:

> Hardy was my poetical father and if I seldom read him now,
> it is, perhaps, because our relationship is so assured as no
> longer to need being made conscious. He is dead, the world he
> knew died too, and we have other roads to build....

> (Auden, 1940, p. 86)

In other words, Hardy, like Auden's own father, belongs to
the past, and has no urgency for the present, no existence,
even, beyond that which we take for granted. Decisively, and
perhaps unwittingly, Auden's confessional mode of justifying
his removal from Hardy (and England?) reinforced the New
Critical sense that what matters in Hardy's poetry has very

little to do with its depiction of the world still recognizable in Auden's 'unsophisticated and provincial' childhood – 'the England of the professional classes, clergymen, doctors, lawyers, and architects...above all a world which had nothing to do with London, the stage, or French literature'(Auden 1940, p. 81). While Hardy's reputation as a poet has, in England, from Edward Thomas to Betjeman, constituted a tradition of localism if not provincialism (see Davie, 1973; Larkin 1983), his standing in the United States has been much more broadly based: not only Ransom and Tate, but also Robert Penn Warren, James Merrill, Harold Bloom, John Hollander and J. Hillis Miller have published work on Hardy that shares little beyond the distinction of its authors. Hardy's poetry has been 'available' to criticism in America while in Britain it remains circumscribed by regional and social considerations. Of the eleven monographs so far published on Hardy's poetry, only three are by British critics; the others are by Americans. Three journals (only one of them British) have devoted special issues to Hardy's poetry: *Southern Review* in 1940, *Agenda* in 1972, and *Victorian Poetry* in 1979. We will look at some of the recent poetry criticism in the next chapter; its listing here serves to stress the 'literary transference' – of Hardy's poetry to America – that Auden, with help from Leavis and I. A. Richards, brought about.

4

The Law of Separation:
Critical Strategies 1940 to the
Present

When in 1963 Albert J. Guerard edited the Hardy volume in
Prentice-Hall's extremely influential series, 'Twentieth Century Views', he acknowledged the importance of *The Southern Review*:

> The very striking impulse of [critics in the 1920s and 30s] was
> to try to make Hardy academically respectable: to insist on
> the formalities and symmetries of his fictional structures, on
> the faithful realism of his picture of Dorset, on the serious-
> ness of his 'philosophy'. These critics tended to apologize for
> the vagaries and eccentricities and audacities of imagining
> that attracts reader today. It may in fact be argued that Hardy
> had to wait until 1940 (with the special and brilliantly edited
> centennial number of *The Southern Review*) for anything like
> an adequate, unpedantic summing-up. It is easy enough to
> demonstrate the importance of this moment in the history of
> Hardy criticism. For these many years afterward I find myself
> drawing upon it for no less than four of the essays for the
> present collection, and there were several others I was
> tempted to use.

(Guerard, 1963, pp. 7-8)

Among those *not* reprinted are the essays by Blackmur, Leavis, Ransom and Tate. Guerard goes on to regret the lack of recent critical activity on Hardy's novels, oddly attributing this to the fact that *The Southern Review* volume had 'covered so much ground', as if criticism were normally an injunction to silence rather than a provocation to join the debate. Guerard also explains the weakness of Hardy criticism in the 1950s by noting that his fiction does not lend itself 'to the methods of the new critics, the formalists, or the delvers into archetype and the psychic underground' (Guerard, 1963, p. 8). Exceptions are made for the essays of Dorothy Van Ghent, John Paterson and A. Alvarez, selected by Guerard for his volume.

One would modify Guerard's point to say that Hardy's fiction did in fact lend itself to New Criticism, and in the process many rather bland assessments were turned out. Hardy's novels were certainly ill-served by the New Criticism but so, one suspects, was any novel more sophisticated than Ford's *The Good Soldier*, that favourite text of 'lazy formalism' and reductive pedagogics. It should be added that while New Criticism was much more appropriate for the study of poetry (the sole focus of its originators), by the 1950s there had set in a dogmatic sclerosis entirely absent from the contributions to *The Southern Review*.

In surveying the critical wasteland between 1940 and 1963 Guerard modestly overlooks his own distinguished contribution in a monograph of 1949. This is marked by frequent comparisons with Conrad and Gide, and by the situating of Hardy in the context of modernity. Guerard's thesis is weakened, however, by the assumption taken over from such contributors to *The Southern Review* as Donald Davidson who, in 'The Traditional Basis of Thomas Hardy's Fiction', treats Hardy as if he were some Homeric epigone like the primitive Yugoslavian shepherds much celebrated at the time by scholars of oral literature: 'He grew up in a Dorset where fiction was a tale told or sung' (Davidson, 1940, p. 166; in Guerard, 1963, p. 13; see also Tate, 1940, p. 101). Throughout this essay runs the assumption that Dorset was somehow impervious to printing. Guerard depends on this caricature to argue against the notion of Hardy as a serious modern philosophical thinker, and against the view, advanced by Beach, Abercrombie and others, that Hardy's novels display aesthetic consciousness and craftsmanship:

> To call him a great craftsman is to do injustice both to these complex and conscientious artists [Flaubert and Turgenev] and to Hardy himself. For we must begin by recognizing that Hardy was pre-eminently a traditional teller of tales, and a great poet who stumbled upon the art of fiction and practiced it very waywardly. We must also recognize that his rich and humane imagination accompanied a plodding and at times even commonplace intellect.
>
> (Guerard, 1949, p. 1)

This condescension is balanced by a modern, or modernist, respect for the primitive, although – as in so many critics of Hardy – it is not clear how exactly, in Hardy, praise and blame are to be apportioned.

Guerard certainly praises Hardy for his acceptance of the horrors of life; for Guerard, Hardy's 'pessimism' is merely a prognosis of the 20th century. One could add that the conscious hypocrisy of the magazine editor's exercise of censorship (conscious in Leslie Stephen, at least) was perpetuated in the criticism that would equate, in Hardy's fiction, degrees of horror with degrees of implausibility. Guerard looks back on Hardy's critics, from Lionel Johnson to Lord David Cecil, and finds that they belong to a 'generation' which is not ours.

> That earlier generation, which I shall call post-Victorian, looked upon its everyday experience as placid, plausible, and reasonably decent.... We now accept Hardy's extreme conjunctions...as highly convincing foreshortenings of the actual and absurd world.
>
> (Guerard, 1949, pp. 2-3)

Guerard's curious use of the word 'plausible' to describe

everyday experience is explained by the later use of 'absurd'; for he argues that Hardy comes into his proper readership with those who have read Kafka, Gide, Conrad and Faulkner. The grotesque and the preposterous are the elements in Hardy for which other critics have apologized; Guerard pays them respectful and illuminating attention.

For some reason, however, Hardy is not to be credited with conscious intention, even though this is certainly not withheld from those such as Conrad, Gide and Kafka, with whom Guerard would make pertinent comparisons. It is not until 1971 that Hardy is acclaimed as a conscious adumbrator of existentialism and absurdism, in Jean R. Brooks' enormously comprehensive and sympathetic study, *Thomas Hardy: The Poetic Structure*. This may still be the only monograph on Hardy entirely free of the note of condescension. And Brooks makes the excellent point that the nonsense perpetrated by Lois Deacon and Terry Coleman in the 1960s about Hardy's doings with Tryphena Sparks and their illegitimate son (for which serious biographers have found no evidence whatever) was really another instance of intellectual censorship and denial: an attempt to explain that Hardy's 'tragic vision' was 'nothing but' an exaggerated and obsessive response to this murky episode. It is not only Deacon and Coleman but also their advocates, and those who would search in the biography for an 'explanation' of so much gloom, who are attempting 'to replace the profound mystery of the suffering artist's creative indictment of the cosmos with a cause small and personal enough for unawakened minds to grasp' (Brooks, 1971, p. 8). For all his talk of modernity and its terrors, one suspects that Guerard has his inhibitions, and remains unable to accept in Hardy what he takes without difficulty in Kafka or Conrad. While he may be right to object to the high place accorded *The Return of the Native* by Beach and Abercrombie, because of its 'formal properties', and to plead for more attention to be given to novels of less obtrusive structure such as *Under the Greenwood Tree* and *The Woodlanders*, it is bad strategy to assume that conscious intention is always productive of forms and structures. 'I do not wish,' declares Guerard, 'to protest against the presence of reasoning in criticism' (Guerard, 1949, p. 9), but he does in effect protest against the presence of reasoning in Hardy's fiction. Guerard's book disappoints because so much of its energy has to be devoted to the avoidance of its own implications. Touching on Hardy's failure to achieve the metaphysical intensities of Dostoevsky, Melville, Conrad and Gide, Guerard takes that failure for granted and offers this in compensation: 'But in our darkening world there is also much to say for Hardy's purity of mind and antique simplicity of art.' This has not the conviction and authority that could stand up against Leavis' scandalous hostility to Hardy in *The Great Tradition*, published the previous year. His infamous words of dismissal (Leavis, 1948, p. 34) do not need to be cited here.

One wonders what is at stake in the image of Hardy, that that 'purity' and 'simplicity' must be retained at any cost. In the 1950s Hardy's reputation seemed secure, if modest, and the modesty was attached to the view of Hardy as historian of Wessex and recorder of rural decline. A useful counter to the dominance of the school of Douglas Brown and Arnold Kettle was to be found in the short but influential essay on *Tess* by Dorothy Van Ghent, first published in 1953: Van Ghent avoids both the sociological and philosophical solutions (which are also dissolutions) without being reductively formalistic.

The work that initiates much of the recent criticism is Roy Morrell's *Thomas Hardy: The Will and the Way* (1965), the first study to make use of such accounts of Hardy's learning and philosophical background as those by Garwood, Rutland and Webster, without subordinating Hardy's texts to philosophical meanings independently arrived at. About *The Dynasts*, for example, Morrell notes that though it has been seldom studied in its own right, it has frequently been quarried for brief quotations that are then taken to hold the key to the novels. Those monographs devoted to *The Dynasts* – J.O. Bailey, *Thomas Hardy and the Cosmic Mind* (1956), Amiya Chakravarty, The Dynasts *and the Post-War Age in Poetry* (1938), Harold Orel, *Thomas Hardy's Epic-Drama: A Study of* The Dynasts (1963), and Walter Wright, *The Shaping of* The Dynasts (1967), find little to comment on apart from the philosophical debate, and even monograph length does not appear to encourage subtlety and discrimination in the analysis. Unlike most critics, who simply ignore *The Dynasts*, Morrell devotes to it a central chapter of his study:

> ...the purpose of this chapter is not just to question the propriety of using *The Dynasts* as a key to the novels... [but] to use our reading of the novels to help elucidate *The Dynasts*; to throw doubt, at least, upon the usual superficial interpretations; to ask whether the human beings in the poem are depicted as always and necessarily puppets of the Will...from many casual critical references, we might infer that *The Dynasts* had nothing to do with human beings at all.
>
> (Morrell, 1965, p. 74)

Morrell's examination of the text of *The Dynasts* and the rest of Hardy's writings reveals little pessimism and even less determinism; instead Morrell finds much compassion, and upbraiding: 'Hardy blames man...for *choosing* to be a puppet' (Morrell, 1965, p. 75). While his reading is scrupulous, and extremely effective at demolishing the notion of monolithic gloom, Morrell sometimes speaks the existentialist language of freedom and choice, but then he relapses into a Victorian earnestness of moral endeavour. Insisting that not everything in Hardy is gloom and despair, Morrell is more inclined to offer sweetness and light than to discriminate among shades of dark grey.

In 1966 Irving Howe prefaced his introductory monograph on Hardy with sentiments hard now to imagine:

> During the last few decades he has been subjected to severe critical attack, at times to blunt dismissal. The novels have suffered most, the poems least; the stories have been ignored. In any case, it can no longer be assumed – it must now be argued – that Hardy is a great writer. Even the most friendly estimates of his work have implied a shift so radical in their terms of appraisal, they have surely left Hardy's more traditional admirers – the vicarious sojourners of Wessex, the

bemused spectators of rusticity, the awed students of philosophy – almost as dismayed as have the attacks.

(Howe, 1966, p. xi)

By 'blunt dismissal' Howe is doubtless referring to Leavis and T.S. Eliot, but in New York he would have been more pressingly aware of the near-silence on the matter of Hardy that was maintained by Lionel Trilling and Edmund Wilson, to name just two of the prominent arbiters of American literary and intellectual life for whom Hardy simply did not figure. It is in that context that one should approach the work of Irving Howe, himself one of the leading contributors since the 1950s to intellectual debate in America.

New Criticism was politically and socially conservative; its concentration on the text ruled out of consideration the circumstances which produced the text, and in which the text was read. Irving Howe, a vociferous socialist of Trotskyite leanings, presents Hardy in what appears to be a reassuringly old-fashioned manner: 'If once you have fallen under the spell...even his minor stories will hold a lively interest' (Howe, 1966, p. 26). And Howe is one of the very few critics to have devoted substantial space and praise to Hardy's short stories. For Howe their value consists in bearing 'hardly a trace of the modern Hardy.... He relaxes into nostalgia and anecdote' (Howe, 1966, p. 77). Howe celebrates 'A Few Crusted Characters', noting that it is ignored by most critics 'eager for philosophical big game'. Howe's favourite, 'one of the great...stories in the English language' (Howe, 1966, p. 82), is 'The Fiddler of the Reels', but its quality has nothing to do with antiquarianism, and is in fact rather 'modern' in its account of the demonic power of music, anticipating Thomas Mann's 'Disorder and Early Sorrow'. (On the short stories, see also Brady, 1982, and Bayley, 1988, pp. 135-48.) We also find Howe attacking the 'gratuitous sophistication' of psychological interpretation, and much more shadow-boxing. Howe's is a particularly frustrating book, for his known ideological and political concerns are so comprehensively masked that it is unclear what Hardy is being used for, or

why he should be the object of Howe's uncharacteristic bland-
ness. Yet we can assume radical purpose in a study of Hardy
that covertly celebrates his lack of popularity in a conservative critical climate.

In 1971, J.I.M. Stewart published *Thomas Hardy: A Critical Biography* which, although entirely free of polemic, presents a thoroughly traditional view of Hardy. Stewart is
always ready to apologize, for Hardy's weak intellect or
repetitive obsessions. It is as if Hardy's reputation needs to
be salvaged, and that this is best achieved by diffidence of
claim and the rhetoric of surrender. Like Howe, Stewart
seems reluctant to explain why the book has been written,
and he offers, I think, no comparison of Hardy with another
writer in which Hardy does not come off worse. If this was
the best that Hardy's advocates could do, against admittedly
formidable opposition, one might have supposed at that time
that Hardy was not destined to be placed among the great
writers.

The revival of Hardy's status can be traced to a few articles
and essays published in the late 1960s and early 1970s,
together with some monographs of the early 1970s that
consolidated the less substantial but more adventurous publications. Tony Tanner's 'Colour and Movement in Hardy's
Tess of the d'Urbervilles' (*Critical Quarterly* x, 1968) is a
brilliant reading of the novel that entirely resists analysis by
character, plot and motivation. This essay had been partially
anticipated by David Lodge whose *Language of Fiction*
(1966) contains a chapter on 'Tess, Nature, and the Voices of
Hardy'. That latter phrase introduces something quite new
in Hardy criticism: the possibility that author and narrator
are not identical, that Hardy may not be answerable for all
the narrator says, is, and commits. Lodge takes up a largely
forgotten attack by Vernon Lee on Hardy, based on a remarkable (for its time) close reading of one passage from ch. 16 of
Tess, of five hundred words. Vernon Lee finds Hardy stylistically wanting, and inconsistent as a narrator, sometimes
telling, sometimes showing, and too often irrelevantly showing off. As an attack on Hardy it has at least the virtue of
precision, and stands independently of any dislike of Hardy's

philosophy or disapproval of his morality.

Lodge takes this attack on its own terms and conditions, and then argues that if there are inconsistencies and confusions of tone and syntax and manner, it is because there is not just one narrative voice. Lodge argues that there are two voices, of the first Hardy and the second Hardy (where we would now of course separate the author entirely from the narrator or narrators), and in a superbly subtle and perceptive analysis he demonstrates the harmonies and dissonances between the voices. In particular, inconsistencies in 'point-of-view' and narrator's or character's consciousnesses need not be smoothed out or explained away but rather justified on the assumption of a plurality of voices. Had Bakhtin been known in the English-speaking world in 1966 there is little doubt that terms such as 'dialogic' would have been invoked. Consequent upon Lodge's essay are various discussions of the narrative voices in Hardy's novels: Schwartz, 1972; Sutherland, 1974; Kramer, 1975; and Lother, 1986. In reviewing Lodge, Millgate (1971) recognized the implications for the reading of '*The Life of Thomas Hardy* by Florence Emily Hardy': 'the Hardy who appears in the *Life* is perhaps engaged in playing the most sustained and richly imagined role of all.' That sense of the narrative sophistication of the *Life* was developed in Millgate's editing and virtual creation of a new book, *The Life and Work of Thomas Hardy*, by Thomas Hardy, published in 1984 and involving theoretical as well as biographical consequences as yet unfathomed.

Equally significant was Lodge's influence on Hillis Miller whose *Thomas Hardy: Distance and Desire* (1970) still remains theoretically the most sophisticated and radical of monographs on Hardy. For Miller there is no 'Hardy himself' but only the many voices he assumes and roles he adopts throughout his writings, and Browning is established as the obvious analogy:

> The narrative voice of Hardy's novels is as much a fictional invention as any other aspect of the story. In fact it might be said to be the most important invention of all, the one which

generates the rest and without which the rest could not come
into existence. The narrator of *The Mayor of Casterbridge* or
The Return of the Native is a role Hardy plays, just as the
characters of Pompilia, Caliban, or Fra Lippo Lippi are roles
Robert Browning plays.... The narrator of *Under the Greenwood Tree* is as much an invented character as is Bishop
Blougram, as much to be distinguished from Hardy as Blougram is from Browning.

(Miller, 1970, p. 41)

Miller is especially concerned to disabuse the reader of the
idea that third-person narration is typically objective and
omniscient. That this supposition should have remained
intact a century after James' theories of narrative consciousness and points of view may be testimony to readers' determination to find Hardy reassuring and old-fashioned. For
Miller it is not all novelists who impersonate narrators but
only those, like Hardy, who possess no character in themselves. That lack is felt to characterize modernity after the
death or disappearance of God: Hardy is thus, in his very lack
of character, representative of the intellectual condition of
his age. As Hardy's writing and his assuming a voice are
always and necessarily simultaneous, Miller is able entirely
to avoid the generic distinction between poetry and fiction.
His study is not generic or stylistic, but thematic, as that
term is understood by the school of phenomenological criticism of which Georges Poulet was the most famous exponent.
Miller analyses and defines the uses of perspective and angle
to create distance, and the function of the look in establishing
desire, in realizing distance as the challenge of difference (see
also Sénéchal-Teissedou, 1980). Meanwhile, the narrators of
poems, novels and stories enact their own dramas of distance,
detachment and longing. Miller has since written two long
essays on *Tess* and on *The Well-Beloved*, collected in *Fiction
and Repetition: Seven English Novels* (1982), and numerous
essays on individual poems ('Wessex Heights', 'In Front of
the Landscape', 'The Torn Letter', 'The Pedigree') which are
as yet uncollected (Miller, 1972, 1985, 1987, 1989). Miller's

conversance with deconstruction, and his background in phenomenology, make his substantive body of critical work on Hardy indispensable for those who would like to see Hardy figuring more prominently (in spite of Miller's prestige) in theoretical debates.

One year after Miller's *Distance and Desire*, Jean Brooks published *Thomas Hardy: The Poetic Structure* (1971). Like Miller, Brooks avoids generic distinctions within the body or 'fabric' of Hardy's writings, and yet avoids the obvious temptation to centre all the writings within the consciousness of an old-fashioned authorial 'Hardy'. The principle of coherence is not to be located in the author but in 'the poetic structure' or even, we might venture, in 'the poetics of structure'. Together with the concern for structure goes a deep involvement with philosophy – not that with which Hardy was familiar but its contemporary manifestation in Existentialism: Camus is a constant point of reference. To read Brooks 20 years on is to understand its tensions as unknowingly marking the development from Existentialism to Structuralism; that no structuralist is cited seems now uncanny. For Brooks, all objections against Hardy based on scepticism about his pessimistic philosophy can now be answered by contemporary apprehensions of the Absurd in Beckett and others (see also Neiman, 1956; Benson, 1984). Unfortunately for Brooks' claims for Hardy, the Absurd (like other continental phenomena) was already out of date when the English discovered it. Moreover, Hardy was so completely identified with Wessex and the decline of rural society that any acknowledgement of his significance as a modern and as a contemporary was strongly resisted.

The third major monograph of the early 1970s, Michael Millgate's *Thomas Hardy: His Career as a Novelist* (1971) is probably the one to have found the most widespread acceptance. Indeed, it set a new standard for Hardy scholarship, further enhanced subsequently by Millgate's biography of 1982 and by Purdy and Millgate's edition in seven volumes of Hardy's *Collected Letters* (1978-88). The professionalism of Millgate's scholarship is matched by the emphasis on Hardy as a professional writer. It was this study that put an

end to Donald Davidson's idea of Hardy as a traditional teller
of tales, and to the generally prevalent notion of Hardy as an
author secluded and spontaneous, uncorrupted by finance
and the machinations of publishing. It is also the first work
since the *Life*, posthumously published in 1928 and 1930, to
add largely and reliably to the biographical data. While the
greatness of Hardy's novels is well appreciated, and endorsed
by extensive critical treatment, this monograph does not
obscure the motive of Hardy's writing. He began in the hope
that he could earn more from fiction than from architecture,
and he had turned to fiction only because he was unsuccessful as a poet. When Hardy stopped writing fiction after *Jude
the Obscure*, he may have done so for a number of reasons,
the most obvious being that he had by that time sufficient
earnings on which to retire comfortably. Millgate's is therefore a 'materialist' reading of Hardy, directing our attention
to the economic circumstances and financial systems within
which novels are not just written by authors but printed,
distributed and read by a network of producers and con-
sumers.

Freed from the obligation to intersperse judicious criticism
within the biographical and textual detail, Millgate in his
biography of 1982 presents a Hardy even more single-minded
in his dedication to a career: 'perhaps no single quality is
more characteristic of Hardy's literary career than his professionalism' (Millgate, 1978, p. 61). Although they barely
acknowledge it (for it is the way of standard works to be taken
for granted) such recent radical approaches to Hardy as those
of George Wotton (1985), N.N. Feltes (1986), John Goode,
(1988) and Peter Widdowson (1989), owe much to the image
of Hardy presented in Millgate's diverse works and editions.

While Hardy's poetry had been given equal status and
generous treatment in the monographs of Miller and Brooks,
it had in general received but a fraction of the critical attention devoted to Hardy's fiction. The first monographs to
concentrate on Hardy's poetry – J.G. Southworth's *The
Poetry of Thomas Hardy* (1947) and Samuel Hynes' *The
Pattern of Hardy's Poetry* (1961) – are almost unbelievably
inadequate as sequels and responses to the essays in *The*

Southern Review of 1940. There is the same withholding of a broad admiration, but nothing of the critical perception of Ransom, Blackmur, Leavis or Tate. Not until 1969 is there a decent monograph, and it must be said that Kenneth Marsden's *The Poems of Thomas Hardy: A Critical Introduction* is, modestly, just that. The first advance on *The Southern Review* came with the special issue of *Agenda*, guest-edited by Donald Davie in 1972. This collection contains two of the most important essays on Hardy's poetry, the editor's 'Hardy's Virgilian Purples' and Thom Gunn's 'Hardy and the Ballads' (now in Gunn's *The Occasions of Poetry*, 1982). Also valuable is John Peck's 'Pound and Hardy', a concise summary of an important but seldom discussed literary relationship. Paul Zietlow's *Moments of Vision: The Poetry of Thomas Hardy* (1974) and Tom Paulin's *Thomas Hardy: The Poetry of Perception* (1975) both attempt to describe the poetry in terms of optical and visual metaphors. Dennis Taylor's *Hardy's Poetry 1860-1928* (1981) and William E. Buckler's *The Poetry of Thomas Hardy* (1983) gesture beyond the introductory. Taylor's recent *Hardy's Metres and Victorian Prosody* (1988) is the most ambitious study yet, for he attributes consciousness and deliberation to every single one of Hardy's poems, and is prepared to regard no poem as accidental or unintended. For the first time in a monograph, Hardy has been accorded the respect that is normally the basis of criticism. One should also mention Donald Davie's peculiar tract, *Thomas Hardy and British Poetry* (1973), in which, embedded in a great deal of extraneous and now very dated material are fifty pages on Hardy's poetry that deserve to be extracted. Some of these studies of the poetry give space to *The Dynasts*, but the most remarkable development is to be found in a three-hundred-page study of *The Dynasts* that gives just one dismissive mention apiece to Schopenhauer and von Hartmann. Susan Dean, in *Hardy's Poetic Vision in* The Dynasts: *The Diorama of a Dream*, proceeds on this courageous and unprecedented premise: 'The assumption that Hardy had an imaginative intention that he accomplished seems at least as plausible as the opposite assumption, and potentially more interesting' (Dean, 1977, p. 3n). It is greatly to be regretted that this book, published by Princeton in 1977, did not provoke the debate that *The Dynasts* sorely requires, nor the upward revaluation that would surely follow. Other treatments of *The Dynasts* deserving mention include Fairley (1919), Dobrée (1940) and Friedman (1988).

Since the 1970s, as before, criticism has continued to be centred on the novels, and if anything, it has become increasingly rigid in its division between major and minor. It was in 1974 that Macmillan for the first time issued in paperback the six 'minor novels', and it might have been hoped that the equal availability of all fourteen of Hardy's novels would encourage a sense of continuum, of that whole cloth which Miller took for the ground of his criticism. Also published in 1974 was Ian Gregor's *The Great Web: The Form of Hardy's Major Fiction*, which takes 'Major Fiction' (the six novels) as a self-evident category. The argument is subtle, and is directed against Henry James' notion of 'form' and what Gregor takes to be its damaging influence on the appreciation of Hardy. Gregor does not take the opposing line and defend the loose, baggy monster but rather seeks to refine the concept of form:

> In Hardy, we find a notion of form, which resides in the structuring power itself, rather than in that which is structured, a sense of form seen not as a result, a shape, more as a process, a direction, a verb rather than a noun.

> (Gregor, 1974, p. 40)

Unfortunately this claim rests here, unsupported by the theoretical work on narrative, and whatever might be meant by the aesthetics of narrative, that has been undertaken in literary theory since the 1960s. It is, furthermore, odd that a critic concerned with the aesthetics of process rather than product should pay such scant, and uncritical, regard to the texts of Hardy's novels. In view of Millgate's chapter on 'The Evolution of Wessex' (1971, pp. 235-48), and of subsequent work by Millgate (1978) and Gattrell (1988), one hardly knows what to make of a chapter-heading: 'The Creation of

Wessex: *Far From the Madding Crowd* (1874)'. While relying on the Wessex Edition throughout, Gregor is trying to argue for a pattern of development, and for an aesthetics of fiction that allows for process and movement. One might also object that Gregor accords to Hardy an aesthetic respectability only by smoothing over or ignoring a great deal (including what Lodge and Miller had noticed), not all of it bad, and some of it of an idiosyncrasy we would not be without.

This may be the nub of the distinction between Hardy's major and minor novels. The major novels are judged so, because they have fewer faults than the minor novels, or because one can ignore certain of their weaknesses without destroying the book: if we ignore the 'weakness' of *A Laodicean* we are left with almost nothing – beyond a first chapter as promising as any in Hardy. David Lodge had initiated a theoretical approach that would have changed those suppositions and certainties. If the narrator is not 'Hardy', then we do not have to blame, excuse or apologize for any of the narrator's weaknesses. Indeed, we can understand the discords, the sheer contrast of tone and style, and also of aesthetic quality, not as blundering somnambulism but as deliberately jarring: representing, if we must cling to the mimetic, the misfittings of things.

Peter Widdowson (1989) spends forty pages in defence of one of the two novels generally regarded as Hardy's worst, *The Hand of Ethelberta* (*A Laodicean* is the other). Aesthetic canons of integrity and unity are modelled on a faith in such a cosmos, and a novel that does not match those criteria will be explained away as a failure. As we have seen, the peculiar chronology of Hardy's 'major' novels, interspersed so arbitrarily among the others, has often been a source of critical wonder. But Widdowson's *Hardy in History: A Study in Literary Sociology* is the first to explain the oddity of that sequence in terms of the inappropriateness of our aesthetic categories. The trouble with this device is that one is tempted to generalize, and to declare any bad book good by other (radical, non-bourgeois) standards. But the conviction in Widdowson's argument derives from our growing awareness that Hardy may always have known what he was doing. In

1980, William Buckler could begin an article thus: 'Critics are discovering daily just what an inestimably subtle man of letters Thomas Hardy really was'(Buckler, 1980). One is very glad that the discovery is being made, but one does speculate whether any other author of modern times has been allowed to languish behind a mask of naiveté for more than 50 years after his death. If the entire critical tradition over the last 100 years has brought us to this discovery, it prompts two sets of questions: how condescending, and gullible, can critics be? And, if the art is in concealing art, what is the proper measurement of concealment, and what now is the measure of what has been uncovered?

From its Aristotelian origins, criticism has been bound to the principles of unity and order. Criticism in its doctrinal and ideological aspect seeks out a coherence of theme, a consistency of cause, intention and teaching. In its aesthetic function, criticism distills multiplicity into unity by seeking for the pattern that is larger than the parts, by projecting a design that leaves nothing out, that allows no component to remain separate except as a flaw. Incoherence, inconsistency, disorganization, shapelessness are attributes of life, whose overcoming is the noble task of art. Horace's notion that art should conceal art indicates the satisfaction that comes with aesthetic realization; as we read, look, apprehend, there is a gradual revelation of order from chaos, of pattern from randomness, of significance from contingency. Much art obviously does not even attempt concealment, and this is labelled not only 'classical' but 'cold', 'formal', even 'inhuman'. It appears to disdain our satisfaction at arriving at the aesthetic, or satisfaction in ourselves at discovering it. By contrast, Hardy's art has always to be uncovered, and the satisfactions that it offers are extraordinarily bound up with the process of reading. While James takes his analogies from architecture, and asks for his art to be admired in the blocks and massings of material as apportioned in part or book, chapter and paragraph, Hardy needs to be read in units seldom more extensive than the sentence. The pleasure of reading James is often to be had in a reflective distance from the text, with a perspective that reconciles character and narrative form; the reader is often in the place of Isabel, in front of the fireplace, contemplating rather than actually reading.

Much criticism of Hardy's fiction has been informed by Jamesian notions of proportionality, of long and short views, of the counterpointing of narrative dynamic with formal stasis. From Beach to Gregor we see the attempt to reclaim Hardy on these terms, and it is this critical tendency that has placed great emphasis on *The Return of the Native* and *The Mayor of Casterbridge*. What such critics mean by 'style' is precisely the sense that every phrase belongs to a unit – 'the complete consort dancing together' – and contributes to 'the overall effect'. Critics such as Vernon Lee have been quite right to attack Hardy's style, and it has been counter-productive for others to point to isolated passages – the Paterian quality of the description of Egdon, for example – as if they were typical or representative. Even David Lodge's defence, by means of disparate narrative voices, depends on a single author behind the narrators who is able to orchestrate the voices and bring harmony out of discord.

Again we must return to *The Southern Review*. The volume's most distinguished contribution to the criticism of Hardy's fiction is Morton Dauwen Zabel's 'Hardy in Defense of His Art: The Aesthetic of Incongruity'. While Zabel's explanations and appeals to historical and social determinants are not entirely satisfying, his description of the case is honest:

> We are never permitted to forget the profound disparity in Hardy's taste and genius, a permanent division between his instinctive attraction toward life and his confusion by it, between his native feeling for words and character and his incurable tendency toward stiff erudition, toward ponderous generalizations on life and experience, toward grandiose symbolism and immensities of scale that wildly exceed the proportions necessary.... There is an essential incongruity in Hardy's world. And he stretched the terms of the incongruity to such a degree that his tales often collapse under the test....Yet in that incongruity, and in what he made of it, lies the secret of Hardy's success.
>
> (Zabel, 1940, pp. 143-4)

It is curious to see how little Zabel can do with his intuition, as if there were no critical method or terminology available for the elaboration of a non-unitary aesthetic. What matters is Zabel's warning against an aesthetic resolution, or reduction of incongruity into homogeneity, and the warning was seldom heeded. Formally, Hardy's novels have been presented as unified entities, with the simple proviso that one exclude novels that restrict coherence and brand them 'minor' or failures.

The ideological, rather than aesthetic, route to unity is to take the inconsistencies and contradictions of Hardy's texts as mimetic of the world: this is the way of Douglas Brown, Raymond Williams and others. Zabel is alert to the possibility of thus misreading Hardy:

> Hardy becomes in his poetics something very different from the victim of scientific determinism that the literal reading of his poems and key-phrases makes him.... His force as a stylist, dramatist, and allegorist is clarified by his refusal to fall in with the restrictions of naturalism, or with an aesthetic based on the rigid and obvious congruities of physical fact.

> (Zabel, 1940, p. 147)

Whether it be 'Wessex' or 'art' or 'technique', Hardy's critics have seldom failed to rest their case on one or other rigid and obvious congruity. The critic's triumph is to take the sprawling profusion of Hardy's texts and uncover a principle of unity and cohesion, all the while assuming that Hardy is being dignified by the exercise.

The difficulty of theorizing the incongruous is, in the abstract, fairly obvious. At the aesthetic level the problem is insoluble as long as one assumes that a work is to be fully appreciated by a single viewer. One can get rid of a single, authorial presence, and accept a text as 'nothing but' a gathering of words and voices, but the 'one' who assumes has already established a unified perspective. The awkwardness of the debate is well illustrated by John Bayley's *The Uses of Division: Unity and Disharmony in Literature* (1976). Hardy receives only casual mentions in a loosely organized argument against 'the usual critical instinct...to show that the work under discussion is as coherent, as aware, as totally organized, as the critic desires his own representation to be' (Bayley, 1976, p. 11). The worth of this thesis – potentially one of the most interesting theoretical developments in recent literary studies – is to be found not in its exposition (necessarily organized) but in its application.

If the best art conceals its art, so the most interesting theories may conceal their own theoretical components. John Bayley's *An Essay on Hardy* (1978) has none of the scholarly or logical organizational trappings: no index, no bibliography, only a dozen footnotes of pointed, parodic inadequacy, no prefatory matter or contents page, no titles or subtitles, and chapter divisions that are merely numerical. For busy scholars it is a most frustrating book that can be read in only one way – from beginning to end. The book's unspoken intent is, we may infer, to be as incoherent, as unaware, as disorganized as the critic desires to show Hardy's texts to be. Unlike other new approaches, this one leads to serious revising of the respective worth of Hardy's works: *Tess* and *Jude* are both found seriously wanting in disunity, and *The Return*, *The Mayor* and *The Woodlanders* are slighted. The single novel to receive the most attention is probably *Desperate Remedies*, with *Two on a Tower*, *A Laodicean* and *The Hand of Ethelberta* all prominently featured. The poems are also scrutinized: a few of the anthologized ones but many more of the obscure and forgettable kind, such as 'The Sunshade' and 'The New Boots'. Once we give up, comprehensively, the aesthetics of unity we find that the reasons why we enjoy reading Hardy, sentence by sentence, have nothing to do with the formal accomplishments of the 'major novels'. Paradox becomes procedure: 'This may sound like a description of weakness rather than strength: I shall try to show it is not'; 'There is then a kind of lukewarmness in the text itself, which is very typical: one can become addicted to it '; 'If he achieves greatness, it is without its outward and visible signs...' (Bayley, 1978, pp. 2, 4, 12).

Bayley elevates Zabel's sense of incongruity into a prin-

ciple of division; it divides not only Hardy's consciousness
into the one who perceives and the one who writes; it also
divides things described from each other, so that no single
thing is conscious of being part of the complete consort. The
scene among the ferns in *Far from the Madding Crowd* 'is
one of the greatest scenes in English fiction' (here Bayley is,
exceptionally, in accord with the critical tradition) because
'it contains all the most original and characteristic elements
of Hardy's style, not fused together but assembled in their
separate peculiarity' (Bayley, 1978, p. 121).

One hesitates to point out the weaknesses of the thesis, for
that would be to expect logic in the representation of that
which makes no claim to the logical. Still, one must assert
that this exceptionally bold theory – brazen in its evaluative
consequences – has a problematic relationship with (or too
straightforward a dependence on) the concept of authorial
intention. It is refreshing to see 'The New Boots' defended on
the grounds, not that its effects are accidental, but that it
fulfils Hardy's intentions completely: 'Of course the effects in
his verse were most carefully calculated' (Bayley, 1978, p. 58).
On the never-before-mentioned poem, 'Expectation and Experience', Bayley enthuses, precisely because it does not
invite our enthusiasm or admiration:

> This is a masterly fiction. There is no apparent intell-
> igence...only an absolute sense of the woman's experience;
> and what brings it before us is not sympathy and perception...
> but a nearly invisible technique that has its firm touch on
> syntax and rhythm, stops and restarts. The remorseless ba-
> nality promised by the title is fully borne out in the text....
>
> The awkward lack of congruence between the last line, and
> its rhyme-partner four lines before, is clearly as deliberate as
> it is effective: Hardy wearied of pointing out that these seem-
> ingly slipshod rhythms were produced by care for a purpose.

> (Bayley, 1978, p. 69)

By contrast a much-admired and anthologized poem such as
'Wessex Heights' is considered by Bayley to be liked for all

the wrong reasons, and chiefly because it resembles a good poem by other poets, such as Belloc or Kipling:

> When Hardy is stung into this kind of bravado he becomes, in a dispiriting sense, like other writers....
>> Yet my love for her in its fulness she herself even did not know;
>> Well, time cures hearts of tenderness, and now I can let her go.
>
> That has not the piercing note of Hardy's rare analysis, but one that is in the bad sense ordinary.

(Bayley, 1979, pp. 67-8)

It requires a very subtle sense to discriminate between the idiosyncratic ordinary of 'The New Boots' and the ordinary ordinary of 'Wessex Heights' – a poem that has struck most readers as anything but ordinary in any sense.

Bayley's argument likewise stumbles over his refusal to acknowledge the greatness of *Tess* and *Jude*; or rather, he concedes their greatness but finds it quite uncharacteristic of Hardy. The argument thus dissipates and wastes its own power by going beyond the brilliant reclamation of the totality of Hardy's writings to a merely provocative inversion of received values. This is unfortunate (and – who knows? – deliberate?) because no other critic has so plausibly explained why we enjoy reading Hardy, and why his 'minor' novels are no less enjoyable than the others. Is it only undiscriminating enthusiasts who want everything, *Tess* as well as *The Hand of Ethelberta*, 'Wessex Heights' as well as 'Expectation and Experience'? Against Bayley's assessments one could note that in part *Tess* and *Jude* are criticized for their total intention and effect, which aspect of, say, *A Laodicean* is simply overlooked in favour of the local detail in the text. The way in which the 'Hardyan law of separation' (Bayley, 1978, p. 74) is compromised in the last novels is itself so complex and subtle that one always suspects that with just one more turn of the view we could see that *Tess* and *Jude* are even better than the other novels, because – let us suppose – their principle of division is even more deviously concealed. The weakness in Bayley's recourse to the intentional fallacy is that the critic can decide that Hardy had the wrong intentions in *Tess* and *Jude*, and there can be no appeal to the evidence, because the evidence can always be handled in a paradoxical manner.

Such reservations are quite beside the main point, which is that the enjoyment of Hardy need no longer be beholden to inappropriate aesthetic standards, and the criticism of Hardy need no longer aim for coherence. As Bayley is regarded as a deeply conservative critic it might be thought odd – were the odd and the obvious not so often one and the same – that *An Essay on Hardy* has had the most far-reaching influence on Marxist, feminist and psychoanalytic readings. It opens the way to an ideological critique that is not to be validated by dialectical resolution.

The movement in the 1980s beyond the positivist project of Douglas Brown, Arnold Kettle and Raymond Williams is heralded in theoretical formulation by James Kincaid whose brief essay, 'Hardy's Absences', on his use of 'the power of absence to effect a brilliantly incoherent art' (Kincaid, 1979, p. 213), should be read in conjunction with 'Coherent Readers, Incoherent Texts' (1977). The debt to Bayley is acknowledged. Having given up on unitary aesthetics and solving ideologies, critics of the 1980s could take what Bayley found to be Hardy's distinctive characteristic and use his divisions to expose the incoherence of unitary readings. It is notable that both Wotton (1985) and Widdowson (1989) include polemical surveys of recent criticism.

George Wotton's *Thomas Hardy: Towards a Materialist Criticism* avails itself of a 'post-dogmatic' Marxism that no longer believes that apparent contradictions are susceptible of 'objective resolution'. Rather than state confidently what Hardy is about, Wotton examines how 'the discourse of aesthetic ideology' produces specific readings of Hardy and how it then constructs 'Thomas Hardy' as 'the author of the ideas upon which these readings are based' (Wotton, 1985, p. 183). This is adequate as a hypothesis, so long as one does not claim the privileged intuition into Hardy's mind that would insist on Hardy's disagreement with 'the discourse of aesthetic ideology'. The critique of aesthetic ideology has a way of assuming that all preferred writers are participants in that critique rather than proponents of that ideology.

The strength of Wotton's position lies in the recognition that aesthetic form is an ideological construct of the reader, not an inherent property of the text. To acknowledge the 'deformation' of Hardy's texts in aesthetic appreciations – appreciations themselves motivated by a desire to prove Hardy's greatness in the only way conventionally acceptable – is to distance oneself from both the aesthetics of unity and the dialectic of reason. Wotton's account of *Jude* locates the hero's 'obscurity' in the virtual impossibility of seeing what is not unified, what has no prospect of being resolved.

> If we see Jude's quest, as the aesthetic project intends we should, as the search for the harmonious conjunction of being and consciousness, then we are obliged to see that what stands in the way of that realization are the ghosts of those superseded forms which refuse to *recognize* him. Wherever Jude turns he finds himself 'left out', literally unseen.
>
> (Wotton, 1985, p. 104)

Jude is, then, a novel designed to fail, both aesthetically and ideologically; as such, it challenges the very procedures of literature. Here a radical concern with the bourgeois origins and determinants of fiction as a social institution – regardless of its explicit 'message' – leads to a position not unlike Bayley's. The worse Hardy is, by conventional standards, and the more clearly he can be shown not to conform to those standards, the better – in his idiosyncratic or radical way – he may be.

John Goode further explores this uncertain terrain ('paradoxical' only from a conventional view-point) in his *Thomas Hardy: The Offensive Truth* (1988). The ambiguity of the title points precisely to the implications of 'aesthetic ideology': if the truth that Hardy tells is truly 'offensive' then the offensive truth may be that Hardy is simply a bad writer. Yet again,

we see developed the strategy of producing a radical Hardy
by taking seriously works that convention has consigned to
'minor' status. Goode's argument is that their failure as
'works of art' is the result of their failure to demonstrate their
explicit thesis. Goode is particularly persuasive on the three
'minor novels' that constitute such a long and inexplicable
lapse between *The Return of the Native* and *The Mayor of
Casterbridge*:

> Hardy attempts to reconstruct a continuity between human
> relationships and a larger wisdom – history in *The Trumpet-
> Major*, 'the march of mind' in *A Laodicean*, the cosmos itself
> in *Two on a Tower*...as we move through the novels, we move
> nearer to the possibility of a new ideological project which
> does not seek wisdom, but seeks to represent instead the
> opposition of structure and agency, the project of the ideologi-
> cal break itself.

(Goode, 1988, p. 65)

Taking the argument one twist further, one could say that
these novels may not have been 'attempts to reconstruct a
continuity' – attempts which fail, and lead Hardy to pursue
another project – but rather attempts to demonstrate the
impossibility of reconstructing *any* continuity. The greatness
of these neglected novels is thus as obscure as Jude himself,
but it is to be identified, as Bayley had demonstrated, in the
phrase, the sentence, the paragraph, and in the fractured
separateness of things out there, of parts of things and of
parts of speech.

The extra twist to Goode's argument is provided by Peter
Widdowson whose lavish defence of *The Hand of Ethelberta*
does not rest its case on the 'significance' of the novel's failure
but insists on its outright success. Some forty pages of Widdowson's *Hardy in History* (1989) are devoted to this novel,
of which Bayley has declared: 'One thing which seems to me
certain is that *Ethelberta* is not a failure: and that it does not
show, as most Hardy critics assume, that he had no sense of
how to handle a social and metropolitan theme. Rather he

had too much sense of it' (Bayley, 1978, p. 153). This 'too much' is what Widdowson teases out:

> By parading the fiction of class, and by articulating this in a fiction which foregrounds its own artifice, *Ethelberta* exposes both how destructive of the individual the class system is...and how illusory is the conception of 'character', of the unitary, efficacious human subject...the novel threatens the coterminous notions of 'the individual' and of 'character' which lie at the heart of bourgeois liberal-humanist ideology and its dominant literary form. 'Artificiality' parallels 'alienation', 'fiction' parallels 'class'; and the character 'Ethelberta' is no more than the amalgam of discourses which structure her in the novel. To ask who is the 'real' Ethelberta, or which is the 'true' story of her life... is to receive the answer: the fictional discourses which determine and represent them – contradictory, discontinuous, fractured, 'unreal'.

> (Widdowson, 1989, p. 196)

The novel which teaches us that lesson is implicitly superior to the novel in which readers can find bourgeois satisfaction. Widdowson would presumably find *Tess* more problematic because it does not prevent its readers from deriving conventional enjoyment, and it offers itself to cinematic and televisual adaptation (on which Widdowson writes with a tone of informed scathing). For Widdowson the 'major novels' are those which everyone reads, and *ought* to have read, out of which 'Wessex' as a symbol of conservative culture is constituted. Their value is now virtually determined by their institutional function in the educational curriculum and in the tourist image of England and Englishness. But, as Widdowson challenges, if we allow his claim for *Ethelberta*, 'why should we assume, then, that Hardy's other fiction is any different?' (Widdowson, 1989, p. 197).

This radical Hardy sits oddly with the biographical data of an ambitious writer, always attentive to financial detail, with social pretensions realized in the building of Max Gate, a thoroughly bourgeois residence, on an elevation overlooking the valley of his modest origins. Equally odd is the feminist fascination with Hardy that has quite abandoned the position of Ellen Moers in 'Tess as Cultural Stereotype', that the novel is full of sexist stereotypes and male fantasies, and should no longer be read. Probably no male author in English literature has been the subject of so much feminist appraisal. And the stance is predominantly well-disposed towards Hardy. While one may discount the extremities in the biographies – notably that by Robert Gittings – Hardy's attitude to women was far from admirable. At the biographical level, there are few less likely candidates among English authors for the kind of prestige that Hardy now commands among politically radical critics.

Even in the 1970s, feminist comment on Hardy was generally unfavourable (see Rogers, 1975), and it could be argued that the dramatic transformation occurred with the breaking down of the ideology of aesthetic unity, and the realization that a text can contain – not as a flaw – diverse and separate strands. Mary Jacobus' articles on Hardy, notably 'Sue the Obscure' (1975) and 'Tess's Purity' (1976), and Elaine Showalter's 'The Unmanning of the Mayor of Casterbridge' (1979) were among the earliest to suspect the complexity that lies just beneath the stereotypes. Yet these essays now seem rather dated, for they argue for parity between the sexes: Sue as much as Jude is the narrative focus of that novel, and Henchard is represented by Hardy as combining both female and male characteristics, and his tragedy is attributed to his unmanning. Patricia Stubbs entitles a chapter of *Women and Fiction* (1979) 'Thomas Hardy, A Study in Contradiction', and the failure to resolve that contradiction is indeed, for Stubbs, Hardy's failure.

Subsequent feminist criticism (see Boumelha, 1982; Morgan, 1988; and Ingham, 1989) has become considerably more sophisticated in its theoretical bearings. Instead of engaging in polemic for the advancement of women to parity with men, or settling for dialectical fantasies of androgyny, feminist criticism has become the site from which 'otherness' and 'difference' are visible. And it is that difference or (in Derrida's special sense) *différance* that offers a social and psychological paradigm for the aesthetics of incongruity and incoherence. The shift that has taken place in the critical application of psychology to literature, from Freud to Lacan, detectable in the English-speaking world since the late 1970s, has been enormously important in this respect. For it has transformed psychology from a branch of medicine (i.e., its work justified by its therapeutic, healing powers) to a branch of philosophy, its work founded on its claims for ontological truth. Among the earliest applications of Lacan to Hardy's fiction are J. Sénéchal-Teissedou's 'Focalisation, regard et désir dans *Far from the Madding Crowd*', and Ramon Saldivar's article, 'Reading the Letter of the Law: Thomas Hardy's *Jude the Obscure*', which uses Lacan's theory of symbolic substitution (of symbols as substitutes) to elaborate that novel's play with the opposition of letter and spirit.

The letteredness of Hardy's text has recently been the subject of numerous essays of semiotic or psychological tendency. Saldivar notes not just letters as epistles but letters as carved, inscribed, engraved, and thus represented in the fictional text. William Harmon (1988) speculates interestingly on the implications of incorporating Gothic lettering, sign-posts and other marks in an otherwise homogeneous text. For here there is no symbolic substitution (i.e., in regular typeface) for the thing represented.

Hardy's Fables of Integrity: Woman, Body, Text by Marjorie Garson (1991) is an attempt to bring together feminist concerns with Lacanian method, and it uncovers the peculiarities of Hardy's text with great clarity and precision. While it has been noticed before that 'parts' of Hardy's characters can take on a separate life as independent entities, and that this anticipates some of the 'shocking' (but conventionally aesthetic) effects of Modernism (as in 'Prufrock'), Garson theorizes this distinctive feature according to Lacan's ideas of mirror-stage identification, castration complex, logocentrism, of identity itself as substitution, of woman as always 'other' to the male who looks and describes. Without in any sense trying to provide a psychological explanation for Hardy's texts, Garson uses divisions and inconsistencies within and between texts to demarcate more forcefully the divisions and disjunctures of the text. Those critics who are determined to read Hardy as 'politically correct' overlook the anxieties that, given his compromised social position, Hardy would have felt, and which are often 'expressed in the novels both in the structure of the fables and in nervously figurative language'. The thesis that is developed along Lacanian lines is that Hardy's text expresses 'somatic anxiety – anxiety about bodily integrity, fear of corporeal dissolution.' The descriptions of nature, the landscape, things out there, are characteristically dependent on the trope of a fragmented human body, and Garson's evidence for this is abundant.

What other critics have done to validate the fragmentary nature of the structure of Hardy's novels, and the conflicts and discontinuities in his representations of history, class, and ideas, and the separations of his syntax, has now been supplemented by Garson's work on the body – of characters, of things, of the text. One is tempted to round things off with a vision of the dialectical progression of Hardy criticism towards some distant resolution. Our one certainty may be that conclusions will always be 'other', and that any claim of integrity and wholeness is an ideological hoax. Conveniently to hand comes *Alternative Hardy*, a collection of essays edited by Lance St John Butler (1989), of which one would give special mention to those by Jean-Jacques Lecercle, Christine Brooke-Rose, Patricia Ingham and Annie Escuret. These essays outline the potential of Hardy criticism, not to illuminate, but to cast shadows marginally lighter than the encircling gloom of our predicament.

Bibliography

(Cross references are marked*)

Abercrombie, L., *Thomas Hardy: A Critical Study* (London, 1912; new edn, 1919)

Agenda, X/i-iii (1972) [Thomas Hardy Special Issue]

Alvarez, A., '*Jude the Obscure*: Afterword'(New York, 1961), repr. *Guerard (1963), pp. 113-22

Auden, W.H., 'A Literary Transference', *Southern Review* (1940), pp. 78-86

Barrell, J., 'Geographies of Hardy's Wessex', *Journal of Historical Geography*, VIII/iv (1982), pp. 347-61

Bayley, J., *The Uses of Division: Unity and Disharmony in Literature* (London, 1976)

———— *An Essay on Hardy* (Cambridge, 1978)

———— *The Short Story: Henry James to Elizabeth Bowen* (Brighton, 1988)

Beach, J.W., *The Technique of Thomas Hardy* (Chicago, 1922)

Beer, G., *Darwin's Plots: Evolutionary Narrative in Darwin, George Eliot, and Nineteenth-Century Fiction* (London, 1983)

Benson, M., 'Moving Bodies in Hardy and Beckett', *Essays in Criticism*, XXXIV/iii (1984), pp. 229-43

Björk, L.A. (ed.), *The Literary Notebooks of Thomas Hardy*, 2 vols (London, 1985)

Blackmur, R.P., 'The Shorter Poems of Thomas Hardy', *Southern Review* (1940), pp. 20-48, repr. in R.P. Blackmur, *Language as Gesture* (New York, 1952), pp. 51-79

Blunden, E., *Thomas Hardy* (London, 1942; new edn, 1951)

Boumelha, P., *Thomas Hardy and Women: Sexual Ideology and Narrative Form* (Brighton, 1982)

Brady, K., *The Short Stories of Thomas Hardy* (New York, 1982)

Brennecke, E.J., *The Life of Thomas Hardy* (New York, 1925)

Brooke-Rose, C., 'Ill Wit and Sick Tragedy: *Jude the Obscure*' in *Butler (1989), pp. 26-48

Brooks, J.R., *Thomas Hardy: The Poetic Structure* (London, 1971)

———— 'The Dynasts as Total Theatre', *Cahiers Victoriens et Edouardiens* (1980), pp. 137-78

Brown, D., *Thomas Hardy* (London, 1954)

Buckler, W.E., 'Thomas Hardy's Sense of Self: The Poet Behind the Auto-biographer in *The Life of Thomas Hardy*', *Prose Studies*, III/i (1980), pp. 69-86

———— *The Poetry of Thomas Hardy: A Study in Art and Ideas* (New York, 1983)

Bullen, J.B., *The Expressive Eye: Fiction and Perception in the Work of Thomas Hardy* (Oxford, 1986)

Butler, L. St John (ed.), *Alternative Hardy* (London, 1989)

Cahiers Victoriens et Edouardiens 12 (1980) [Studies in Thomas Hardy]

Cecil, Lord David, *Hardy the Novelist: An Essay in Criticism* (London, 1943)

Chase, M.E., *Thomas Hardy: From Serial to Novel* (Minneapolis, 1927)

Chew, S.C., *Thomas Hardy: Poet and Novelist* (New York, 1921)

Child, H., *Thomas Hardy* (London, 1916)

Cox, R.G. (ed.), *Thomas Hardy: The Critical Heritage* (London, 1970)

Davidson, D., 'The Traditional Basis of Thomas Hardy's Fiction', *Southern Review* (1940), pp. 162-78

Davie, D., 'Hardy's Virgilian Purples', *Agenda* (1972), pp. 138-56

———— *Thomas Hardy and British Poetry* (London, 1973)

Dean, S., *Hardy's Poetic Vision in* The Dynasts: *The Diorama of a Dream* (Princeton, 1977)

Deleuze, G., and Parnet, C., *Dialogues* (French edn, 1977), tr. H. Tomlin-son, and B. Hammerson, (London, 1987)

Dobrée, B., 'The Dynasts', *Southern Review* (1940), pp. 109-24

Duffin, H.C., *Thomas Hardy: A Study of the Wessex Novels, the Poems and* The Dynasts (Manchester, 1916; third edn, 1964)

Elliott, G.R., 'Hardy's Poetry and the Ghostly Moving-Picture', *South Atlantic Quarterly* 27 (July 1928), pp. 280-91

———— 'Spectral Etching in the Poetry of Thomas Hardy', *Publications of the Modern Languages Association*, XLIII/ii (1928), pp. 1185-95

Elliott, R.W.V., *Thomas Hardy's English* (Oxford, 1984)

Ellis, H., 'Thomas Hardy's Novels', *Westminster Review* (April, 1883)

Enstice, A., *Thomas Hardy: Landscapes of the Mind* (London, 1979)

Escuret, A., 'Tess des d'Urberville': le Corps et le Signe', *Cahiers Victoriens et Edouardiens* (1980), pp. 85-136

———— 'Thomas Hardy and J.M.W. Turner' in *Butler (1989), pp. 205-25

Fairley, B., 'Notes on the Form of *The Dynasts*', *Publications of the Modern Languages Association* 34 (1919), pp. 401-15

Feltes, N.N., *Modes of Production of Victorian Novels* (Chicago, 1986)

Firor, R.A., *Folkways in Thomas Hardy* (Philadelphia, 1931)

Friedman, B.A., *Fabricating History: English Writers on the French Revolution* (Princeton, 1988)

Garson, M., *Hardy's Fables of Integrity: Woman, Body, Texts* (Oxford, 1991)

Garwood, H., *Thomas Hardy: An Illustration of the Philosophy of Schopenhauer* (Philadelphia, 1911)

Gatrell, S., *Hardy the Creator: A Textual Biography* (Oxford, 1988)

Gittings, R., *Young Thomas Hardy* (London, 1975)

———— *The Older Hardy* (London, 1978)

Goode, J., *Thomas Hardy: The Offensive Truth* (Oxford, 1988)

Graves, R., *Goodbye To All That* (London, 1927; new edn, 1960)

Gregor, I., *The Great Web: The Form of Hardy's Major Fiction* (London, 1974)

Grimsditch, H.B., *Character and Environment in the Novels of Thomas Hardy* (London, 1925)

Grundy, J., *Hardy and the Sister Arts* (London, 1979)

Guerard, A.J., *Thomas Hardy* (Cambridge, MA, 1949; new edn, New York, 1964)

———— (ed.), *Hardy: A Collection of Critical Essays* (Englewood Cliffs, 1963)

Gunn, T., 'Hardy and the Ballads', *Agenda* (1972), pp. 19-46, repr. in T. Gunn, *The Occasions of Poetry* (London, 1982), pp.77-105

Hardy, F.E., *The Life of Thomas Hardy* (London, 1962)

Harmon, W., 'Only a Man: Notes on Thomas Hardy', *Parnassus*, XIV/ii (1988), pp. 287-309

Hickson, E., Cathcart, *The Versification of Thomas Hardy* (Philadelphia, 1931)

Hollander, J., *The Figure of Echo* (Berkeley, CA, 1981)

———— 'Breaking into Song: Some Notes on Refrain', in (eds) C. Hosek and P. Parker, *Lyric Poetry: Beyond the New Criticism* (Ithaca, NY, 1985), pp. 73-89

Holloway, J., *The Victorian Sage: Studies in Argument* (London, 1953)

———— *The Charted Mirror* (London, 1960)

Howe, I., *Thomas Hardy* (New York, 1966)

Hyman, V.R., *Ethical Perspective in the Novels of Thomas Hardy* (New York, 1975)

Hynes, S., *The Pattern of Hardy's Poetry* (Chapel Hill, NC, 1961)

Ingham, P., *Thomas Hardy* (Brighton, 1989)

———— 'Provisional Narratives: Hardy's Final Trilogy', in *Butler (1989), pp. 49-73

Jacobus, M., 'Sue the Obscure', *Essays in Criticism*, XXV/iii (1975) pp. 304-28

———— 'Tess's Purity', *Essays in Criticism*, XXVI/iv (1976), pp. 318-38

James, H., *Literary Criticism: Essays on Literature, American Writers, English Writers* (New York, 1984)

Johnson, L., *The Art of Thomas Hardy* (London, 1894; new edn, 1928)

Johnson, T., ' "Pre-Critical Innocence" and the Anthologist's Hardy', in *Victorian Poetry* (1979), pp. 9-29

Kay-Robinson, D., *Hardy's Wessex Re-appraised* (Newton Abbot, 1972)

Kettle, A., *Hardy the Novelist* (Swansea, 1966)

Kincaid, J.R. 'Coherent Readers, Incoherent Texts', *Critical Inquiry*, III (1977), pp. 781-802

———— 'Hardy's Absences' in *Kramer (1979), pp. 202-13

Kramer, D., *Thomas Hardy: The Forms of Tragedy* (Detroit, 1975)

———— (ed.), *Critical Approaches to the Fiction of Thomas Hardy* (London, 1979)

Larkin, P., *Required Writing: Miscellaneous Pieces 1955-82* (London, 1983)

Lawrence, D.H., *Study of Thomas Hardy and Other Essays*, (ed.) B. Steele (Cambridge, 1985)

Lea, H., *Thomas Hardy's Wessex* (London, 1913)

Leavis, F.R., *New Bearings in English Poetry* (London, 1932; new edn, 1963)

———— 'Hardy the Poet', *Southern Review* (1940), pp. 87-98

———— *The Great Tradition* (London, 1948; new edn, 1962)

Lecercle, J.J., 'The Violence of Style in *Tess of the d'Urbervilles*' in *Butler (1989), pp. 1-25

Lee, Vernon, *The Handling of Words* (London, 1922)

Lerner, L., and Holmstrom, J. (eds), *Thomas Hardy and His Readers* (London, 1968)

Lipking, L., *The Life of the Poet: Beginning and Ending Poetic Careers* (Chicago, 1981)

Lodge, D., *Language of Fiction: Essays in Criticism and Verbal Analysis of the English Novel* (London, 1966)

———— 'Thomas Hardy and Cinematographic Form', *Novel* 7 (1973-4), pp. 246-54

Lothe, J., 'Hardy's Authorial Narrative Method in *Tess of the d'Urbervilles*' in (ed.) J. Hawthorn, *The Nineteenth-Century British Novel* (London, 1986), pp. 157-70

Macdonell, A., *Thomas Hardy* (London, 1894)

McDowall, A., *Thomas Hardy: A Critical Study* (London, 1931)

Marsden, K., *The Poems of Thomas Hardy: A Critical Introduction* (London, 1969)

Miller, J. Hillis, *Thomas Hardy: Distance and Desire* (Cambridge, MA, 1970)

———— 'History as Repetition in Thomas Hardy's Poetry: The Example of "Wessex Heights" ', in *Victorian Poetry*, Stratford-upon-Avon Studies, 15 (1972), pp. 223-53

———— *Fiction and Repetition: Seven English Novels* (Cambridge, MA, 1982)

———— 'Thomas Hardy, Jacques Derrida, and the "Dislocation of Souls" ', in (eds) J.H. Smith and W. Kerrigan, *Taking Chances: Derrida, Psychoanalysis and Literature* (Baltimore, 1984), pp. 135-45

———— 'Topography and Tropography in Thomas Hardy's *In Front of the Landscape*', in (eds) M.J. Valdes and O. Miller, *Identity of the Literary Text* (Toronto, 1985), pp. 73-91

———— 'Prosopopoeia in Hardy and Stevens' in *Butler (1989) pp. 110-27

Millett, K., *Sexual Politics* (London, 1969)

Millgate, M., *Thomas Hardy: His Career as a Novelist* (London, 1971)

———— 'Hardy's Fiction: Some Comments on the Present State of Criticism', *English Literature in Transition*, XIV/iv (1971), pp. 230-8

'The Making and Unmaking of Hardy's Wessex Edition' in (ed.) J. Millgate, *Editing Nineteenth-Century Fiction* (New York, 1978)

———— *Thomas Hardy: A Biography*, (Oxford, 1982)

———— (ed.), *The Life and Work of Thomas Hardy by Thomas Hardy*, (London, 1984)

Mizener, A., '*Jude the Obscure* as a Tragedy', *Southern Review* (1940), pp. 193-213

Moers, E., 'Tess as a Cultural Stereotype' in (ed.) A.J. LaValley, *Twentieth-Century Interpretations of* Tess of the d'Urbervilles (Englewood Cliffs, 1969)

Morgan, R., *Women and Sexuality in the Novels of Thomas Hardy* (London, 1988)

Morrell, R., *Thomas Hardy: The Will and the Way* (Kuala Lumpur, 1965)

Murfin, R.C., *Swinburne, Hardy, Lawrence, and the Burden of Belief* (Chicago, 1978)

Murry, J.M., *Aspects of Literature* (London, 1920)

Neiman, G., 'Thomas Hardy, Existentialist', *Twentieth-Century Literature*, I/iv (1956)

Orel, H. (ed.), *Thomas Hardy's Personal Writings* (Kansas, 1966)

Paterson, J., '*The Mayor of Casterbridge* as Tragedy', *Victorian Studies* III (1959), pp. 151-72

Paulin, T., *Thomas Hardy: The Poetry of Perception* (London, 1975)

Peck, J., 'Pound and Hardy', *Agenda* (1972), pp. 3-10

Purdy, R.L., *Thomas Hardy: A Bibliographical Study* (Oxford, 1954)

Purdy, R.L., and Millgate, M. (eds), *The Collected Letters of Thomas Hardy* (seven vols, Oxford, 1978-88)

Ransom, J.C., 'Honey and Gall', **Southern Review* (1940), pp. 2-19

Richards, I.A., *Science and Poetry* (London, 1926)

———— 'Some Notes of Hardy's Verse Forms', *Victorian Poetry* (1979), pp. 1-8

Rogers, K.M., 'Women in Thomas Hardy', *Centennial Review* 19, (1975), pp. 249-58

Rutland, W.R., *Thomas Hardy: A Study of His Writings and Their Background* (Oxford, 1938)

Saldivar, R., *Figural Language in the Novel* (Princeton, 1984)

Schwartz, D., 'Poetry and Belief in Thomas Hardy', *Southern Review* (1940), pp. 64-77

Schwartz, D.R., 'The Narrator as Character in Hardy's Major Fiction', *Modern Fiction Studies* XVII (1972)

Sénéchal-Teissedou, J., 'Focalisation, regard et désir dans *Far from the Madding Crowd*', in *Cahiers Victoriens et Edouardiens* (1980), pp. 73-84

Showalter, E., 'The Unmanning of the Mayor of Casterbridge', in **Kramer* (1979), pp. 99-115

Snell, K.D.M., 'Thomas Hardy, rural Dorset, and the family', in *Annals of the Labouring Poor: Social Change and Agrarian England 1660-1900* (Cambridge, 1985), pp. 374-410

The Southern Review, VI/i (1940) [Thomas Hardy Centennial Issue]

Southworth, J.G., *The Poetry of Thomas Hardy* (New York, 1947)

Stewart, J.I.M., *Thomas Hardy: A Critical Biography* (London, 1971)

Stubbs, P., *Women and Fiction: Feminism and the Novel 1880- 1920* (Brighton, 1979)

Sutherland, J., 'A Note on the Teasing Narrator in *Jude the Obscure*', *English Literature in Transition* 17 (1974), pp. 159-62

Tanner, T., 'Colour and Movement in Hardy's *Tess of the d'Urbervilles*', *Critical Quarterly* X (1968)

Tate, A., 'Hardy's Philosophic Metaphors', in **Southern Review* (1940), pp. 99-108

Taylor, D., *Hardy's Poetry, 1860-1928*, (London, 1981)

———— *Hardy's Metres and Victorian Prosody* (Oxford, 1988)

Taylor, R.H. (ed.), *The Personal Notebooks of Thomas Hardy* (London, 1978)

Vaché, J., 'Structures metaphoriques dans *Les Dynastes*' in *Cahiers Victoriens et Edouardiens* (1980), pp. 179-200

Van Ghent, D., 'On *Tess of the d'Urbervilles*' (1953), repr. in *Guerard (1963), pp. 77-90

Victorian Poetry, XVII/i-ii (1979) [The Poetry of Thomas Hardy: A Commemorative Issue]

Wain, J., 'Introduction' to Thomas Hardy, *The Dynasts* (London, 1965)

Webster, H.C., *On a Darkling Plain: The Art and Thought of Thomas Hardy* (Chicago, 1947)

Widdowson, P., *Hardy in History: A Study in Literary Sociology* (London, 1989)

Williams, M., *Thomas Hardy and Rural England* (London, 1972)

Williams, R., *The Country and the City* (London, 1973)

────── *The English Novel from Dickens to Lawrence* (London, 1970)

Woolf, V., *The Second Common Reader* (London, 1932; new edn, 1944)

Wotton, G., *Thomas Hardy: Towards a Materialist Criticism* (Goldenbridge, Eire, 1985)

Zabel, M.D., 'Hardy in Defense of His Art: The Aesthetic of Incongruity', in *Southern Review* (1940), pp. 125-49

Zietlow, P., *Moments of Vision: The Poetry of Thomas Hardy* (Cambridge, MA, 1974)

Index